I did my best, it wasn't much.
I couldn't feel, so I learned to touch.
I've told the truth, I didn't come to fool you.
And even though it all went wrong,
I'll stand before the Lord of Song
with nothing on my lips but Hallelujah

(gratefully excerpted from
Hallelujah by Leonard Cohen)

INTERGENERATION LOST AND FOUND

why suits and skirts don't talk with jeans,

why they should, and how they can

Harry A. Van Belle

Legacy Press 2012

flat 3rd & 5th
note of
I = IV (#IV dim chord) -V
|
aug - raise
the 5th.) biggest

I - V (over the - VI minor -
F# in base.

Published in 2012 by Legacy Press
10517 69 Street
Edmonton, Alberta
Canada T6A 2S7
harryvanbelle@hotmail.com

Printed by Create Space

$I - V/ii - I/iii - IV - {}^{\#}iv^{o7} - I/V$

- ii mi

CONTENTS

Jeans, Suits and Skirts

What's with these young kids in jeans camped out in public parks all over North America, shouting occupy this and occupy that? There's hardly any of them over 30 in the lot. Shouldn't they be in school or working or something? Don't they know that winter is upon us and they could freeze to death? They are not really homeless, are they? They have warm places to go to. Why don't they just pack up and leave?

It is indeed a crying shame that these young people are left with no other form of protest to get their voices heard by the politicians and pundits who run the world. As it is, grownup men and women in suits and skirts, who are most often the parents of the kids camped out, appear to have no clue why their children are so upset. Nor do they seem to care. The best they offer them is condescendence and disdain.

In the mean time the world is going to hell in a hand basket, while the ones in the know, the suits and the skirts, seem powerless to stop it. That scares these young kids in jeans enough to camp out in the cold. But no one is listening to them and that is a terrible tragedy, because these young people's actions are the voices of our tomorrow.

"If only they would more clearly tell us what they want!" we hear time and again. And that is so much nonsense, because it is crystal clear what they want. They want an end to a system where it is normal for one to better him or herself at the expense of their neighbour and a start to a system where each of us is busy being our next-door neighbour's keeper. Now, don't ask these kids in jeans how to put this into practice. That is a job for us suits and skirts.

Written in solidarity with the Occupy Wall Street movement (Oct. 2011)

Preface[1]

After two years of talking, listening, and reading anything I could about young people in their twenties I have been forced to conclude that suits like me don't understand anything about jeans like the occupiers. People older than let's say 40 have no clue of what's going on with people younger than let's say 30.

That should not surprise me. I am 75 years old and there is a half a century between me and these kids in jeans. That's a distance of twice their age! Whatever I can realistically hope to know about them I can only know from the outside in, never from the inside out.

My surprise has to do with something else. I really like these young people. I like being with them. And they with me, it seems. But they are not like me. They are different. From my perspective they are wonderfully weird. I dare say that this is how anyone over forty feels about anyone under 30. The generations don't *get* one another because they are just not *like* one another. In the words of one parent: "Trying to understand our twenty-something son or daughter, is much like immigrating to a strange country. We neither know our children's language nor their customs." That was already the sentiment of Margaret Mead in 1971! She stated that because of the rapid pace of change in our culture younger and older people live in different worlds.

It's not as if the generations hate one another. They just live alongside one another like two solitudes. There exists a profound intergenerational disconnect between parents and children, teachers and students, employers and employees in our world today.

Perhaps the most fundamental way in which young people differ from older folk is that their lives are by and large characterized by what someone called " the integrity of questioning rather than the certainty of knowing." Theirs is a probing generation. They view testing things out as an authentic place to stand. They like to live on the edge, to try new things, to walk in a space of not knowing, and to believe something tentatively for the time being to see where it leads them. They are receptive to otherness, welcoming of diversity, open to dialogue, willing to be taught and ready to change their minds.

They believe that all points of view are inevitably subject to revision and doubt that there are many prefabricated truths worthy to live by.

By way of contrast, their parents, their teachers and their employers have a stake in maintaining that some things must be true no matter what. They feel uncomfortable with so much openness and uncertainty. They tend to trust the validity of scientifically established facts more than their children and value historically established patterns of living. It has taken them years to craft a credible way of living of their own and they feel that their life style is currently under attack. They secretly want their children to adopt their values and their life style, to accept their worldview and follow in their footsteps but see very little evidence that this is happening. In my experience it is troubling for many parents to watch their children's lives go in a direction that is quite different from their own.

Setting the stage

This book represents a study of young people between 18 -30, the so-called emerging adult generation, and of the way they interact with members of older generations. It contains a series of items, each intended to describe what I perceive to be a central characteristic of the life style and experience of this age group. Of course the lives of these post-adolescent semi-adults are far more complex than can be captured in the description of any one characteristic. It is only through the cumulative portrait of all these items combined that it may become evident what these young people are all about. Together these items can be likened to individual strands in a multi-coloured scarf my wife likes to knit in her spare time.

Furthermore, the items are grouped into six chapters to highlight the broader dimensions of the experience and life style of emerging adults. Chapter one deals with basic characteristics of emerging adulthood. Chapter two describes the way these young people interact with information technologies, the impact of which is so pervasive in their lives. Chapter three tells the story of a subgroup of emerging adults, the so-called hipsters, to highlight the place of irony in the lives of today's young people. Chapter four chronicles the way this emerging generation interacts and communicates with preceding generations. Then follows chapter five in which I attempt to place this generation historically in relation to post-modernism. Lastly, the book ends with some concluding personal postscripts about what this all means for the way we intergenerationally live together in the twenty-first century.

Chapter One:

EMERGING ADULTHOOD[2]

On being twenty-something in the 21ˢᵗ Century (20+/2012)

1. Emerging

People in their twenties are said to be *emerging*. We do not say that about any other age group in life. But for about a decade that is what these semi-adults appear to be doing. They are emerging. It is the first characteristic that uniquely depicts their lives. Development *defines* their existence. They are perpetually on the way. They live lives in transition. Their lives are in flux; everything about them is fluid and dynamic. They move from place to place and from time to time. They leave home to move to college, in college they typically change their majors a number of times, at work they never stay long in any one job, in the social arena they change friends, lovers, partners, relationships more than once and they tinker with their worldview or life perspective throughout their twenties.

They are perpetual motion machines. They see themselves as a work-in-progress. They are constantly going somewhere but without the certainty that they will ever arrive. Their lives are transitory. Everything is for the time being only. Nothing is settled. Everything is still up for grabs. But then, everything is also still possible for them. Who knows?

2. In between

We all live our lives in between what is no longer and what is not yet.
But being in between defines the lifestyle of today's young people in
their twenties. For about a decade they live in between the
dependence of adolescence and the dependability of adulthood.
Emerging adulthood is a historically new developmental stage in the
life span. The previous generation (today's parents, teachers and
employers) never had to deal with this period of emerging. They
moved directly from adolescence into young adulthood. Which may
be why they want today's young people to get on with it and to grow
up. But for all sorts of historical reasons today's young people have
no choice but to spend a lengthy time emerging into adulthood.
Living in between lives for a time is developmentally inescapable for
them. That first of all.

Second, this in between life is also a period of uncertainty. For about
a decade they live their lives between a childhood certainty and an
adult certainty. As children these young people accepted what their
adults told them and that settled the matter. What they had was an
unquestioned certainty. They could be sure about something if mom,
or dad or the teacher said so. That all changed during adolescence
when they developed the ability to think for themselves. This led
them to question the validity of their childhood certainties, which
was a healthy process because this questioning formed a necessary
bridge between the innocence of their childhood and the formation
of a more realistic adult outlook on life. For most of their parents
this shift to an adult outlook on life occurred in late adolescence or
early twenties. But most of today's young people do not arrive at this
new understanding of life until their late twenties or early thirties.
Their questioning continues for another decade, which predisposes
them to live in between lives.

Third, young people generally use the experience of their parents as a
template for finding their own way. Stories about what their parents
experienced during their twenties and how they behaved form a kind
of prototype for what they can expect and how they should behave.
But, their parents' experience of life in their twenties was in many
ways substantially different from the challenges facing today's

emerging adults. Their parents needed less education, had more job security and married earlier than today's young people. All this leaves these twenty-somethings without a roadmap on the way to adulthood. Even if they wanted to do no more than imitate the developmental trajectory of their parents they could not. The map and the territory do not match. This is yet another way in which they are compelled to live in between lives.

Finally, the personal development of individuals is greatly influenced by the cultural-historical unfolding of the society in which they live. This is true also for the development of today's emerging adults. However, they have the misfortune of living their youth at a time in history when society is in the process of exchanging one generally accepted outlook (modernism) on life for another (postmodernism). It is clear to many people in the know today that the old ways of looking at life are no longer adequate to the challenges of the day. However, it is not at all clear to them what world and life view should take its place. In the words of Arthur Zajonk: " The old forms rattle and the new delay to appear." The tragedy of today's emerging adults is that they were "born too late for the old and too early for the new faith."[3]

3. Homeless

Young people usually leave home at the start of their twenties. In that sense they become homeless, i.e. cut off from the place in which they were born and not settled in the place in which they will spend their future. But there is another, perhaps even more profound sense in which they become homeless. In our culture they are considered to be adults at 21. No one will tell them any longer what to do, when to get up, what to eat, how to keep house or what to live *for*. They can be single, married, cohabit, go to school, or not, live anywhere in the world, and believe, doubt, or question anything they want. They are given much freedom of choice and little is expected of them except that they make their life choices on their own.

In addition, today's emerging adults are faced with an overwhelming overload of choice. To give just one example, they have over 800,000 possible careers to choose from. That can make deciding on a life's vocation a daunting task. Making decisions in the other areas of their life like whom to marry, where to live or what philosophy of life to commit themselves to is no easier for them in today's world.

With all the privileges they enjoy these young people frequently express feeling a deep sense of existential loneliness. In the absence of mentors helping them find their way, they are often at a loss what to do or where to turn. They experience the world as an unpredictable, foreign place in which they do not feel at home and it is hard for them to make up their individual minds.

What young people experience most today is a dearth of ends rather than means. They are smart enough to get from A to B, provided that they would know why they should go there. They often lack a vision for the future and no one is inspiring them. "I wish that someone would tell me how to live my life", one emerging adult exclaimed recently. "I would like to be a fish in a fish bowl: open to the world outside, but safe in the water, protected by the bowl."[4]

We live in a world where there is a plurality of vision. Truth has become a matter of opinion, of how you look at it. What's true for me may not be true for you. In a world in which there is an absence of indubitable facts *and* of over-riding values it is easy to feel homeless.

4. It's all up to me but who am I?

Emerging adulthood is a time of searching for concrete answers to big questions. Faced with the necessity of mapping out their future and in the absence of contextual support on how to do that, the only person emerging adults can turn to for answers is themselves. Finding their way in life becomes a lengthy do-it-yourself project.

Discovering what life is all about for these young people begins with finding out who they are and what they can do. This is another defining characteristic for these emerging adults. At the start of their twenties they, by their own admission, don't know who they are, what they can do or what they should be doing with their lives. The famous philosopher Rene Descartes wrote centuries ago *cogito ergo sum,* "I think, therefore I am." Today's emerging adults are more likely to exclaim with some frustration: "I think and think, and think, but I still don't know who I am!" Discovering what life is all about for these young people begins with discovering their identity. Identity exploration takes up much of their time and effort during their twenties.

5. Searching for self in work and love

When asked about the meaning of life, the psychoanalyst Sigmund Freud replied *Arbeiten und Lieben*, working and loving. It is in these two areas of their life, in career preparation and in their search for meaningful relationships, that today's emerging adults explore their identity. These are the areas in which they want to find out who they are and what can be expected of them.   And the end product of this search is ideally that they have learned: 1) to take responsibility for themselves, 2) to make their own decisions, and 3) to become (financially) self-sufficient. These are what they believe to be the marks of being an adult. It is only after they have achieved these three goals that they feel responsible enough to enter a committed relationship with a life partner, to marry and to start a family.

In searching for a suitable career they want to discover what sort of work they find satisfying, what sort of work they are good at and what sort of work gives them the best chance of remaining gainfully employed throughout their life.

So, in the area of educationally preparing themselves for a career they may change their major in university a number of times in order to be well prepared. Then, once they graduate, they usually try out a number of jobs, all of them aimed at laying the groundwork for their life's vocation.

6. Identity precedes intimacy

In the area of love emerging adults engage in a number of different romantic relationships, the goal of which is to get an answer to the question: "Given that I am this sort of person, what sort of person would suit me as my life partner?" This search for an identity in love relationships can take quite a while. Today's twenty-something young people most often do not get married until their late twenties or early thirties. In this the current generation differs from their parents, most of who married in their early twenties.

Furthermore, for them identity formation takes precedence over establishing a committed, intimate relationship with another emerging adult. For a time the relationships they do form, whether romantic or friendship, are of necessity fluid and focused on the job of identity exploration. This even holds for the relationships they form in order to make a choice in a marriage partner. They may prefer to live together with someone to discover what it is like to be married *before* they actually marry. Cohabitation is a less committed form of living together and fits the for-the-time-being character of emerging adulthood.

7. Emerging adults and their iPhones: why friends are important

Friendship relations are also governed by a focus on identity formation for emerging adults. Away from home and family, emerging adults use meeting and living with friends mostly as a substitute for family life. Friends provide them with social stability and some sense of community. They look for friends any place they can find them, via online dating, through facebook, or via text messaging. Through these means of computer technology they participate in a virtual community. They are linked with other emerging adults through social networking, via email, blogging and twitter. But it is all for the time being only as they vacillate between their need for identity and their need to belong, between becoming themselves and becoming connected.

This fact needs some historical contextualization. One major historical change over the last half-century is the explosion of information technology. Its impact is especially evident among emerging adults. They have whole-heartedly embraced all things digital and are the most tech savvy generation of all times. This is another one of the characteristics that distinguishes them from previous generations. The availability over the last several decades of personal computers, wirelessly connected laptops and cell phones or mobiles has given them access to the internet, email services, and information search engines like Google. These instant information and communication technologies have easily made them the most informed and connected generation in history. In addition, a vast array of social networking sites like facebook, my space, twitter and YouTube are at their disposal. Emerging adults have enthusiastically taken these communication gadgets into their bosom and like prostheses have made them into extensions of their bodies. I am told by many of them that they sleep with their cell phones on so that they can be on line 24/7.

All this has made them the most peer-oriented generation in history, as is evidenced by the high importance they place on unchecked self-expression and on the unconditional acceptance of self-expression by others via these social networking services. Many emerging adults post personal profiles and videos of themselves on the net and update their status regularly. They also avidly scrutinize and comment on the profiles of their many network friends. They hunt the net for interesting videos and noteworthy tidbits of information and pass them on to their friends. They text one another continually about the most mundane events of their day-to-day lives. "I just had a lovely oatmeal breakfast." "I had eggs on toast." They spend a lot of their time emailing, blogging, or tweeting their opinions about anything in the world to their network friends. All this in an attempt to provide a social- relational context, so necessary in their decade-long search for an identity.

8. Crafting an interpersonal faith inside a plurality of vision

Globalization has made today's world increasingly into a single place where we are all exposed to a wide variety of worldviews, cultures, ideologies and religions. In such a world all ideologies, religions and cultures tend to become relativized. Nothing is true no-matter-what anymore. More and more we are faced with the fact that there is more than one kind of normal in the world. The otherness of others is in our face all the time. In such a world it is hard to escape the notion that we all make our philosophy of life or our religion what it is, that what we believe is strictly up to us, and that there is no longer any overarching system of truth out there to appeal to.

Emerging adults are keenly aware of this situation. Rather than search for a worldview that we can all share, the thing that concerns them most is the quality of their character. What counts for them is the ability to make their own choices and to live by them, the willingness to take responsibility for themselves, and the commitment to live honest and authentic lives. They have by and large exchanged the certainty of knowing for the integrity of questioning. They have come to believe what they believe without the pretension that what they believe is the only truth. They show respect for the fact that others may have a faith that differs from theirs. They develop an ultra-tolerant interpersonal faith, which says that whatever you believe, above all it must not hurt others or make them feel put down. The faith they do profess to have is a kind of open spirituality in which they pick and choose what to believe. What to live out of and what to live for are private, individual matters. In the words of one emerging adult, they have become a congregation of one.

9. The hopefulness of emerging adulthood: All is still possible when nothing is decided

If one thing is surprising about emerging adults it is how optimistic they are. Given all that is happening to them one would expect them to be dejected. Instead they are uncommonly hopeful for their personal future. They are generally upbeat, full of dreams and wide-open to change. What might be the explanation for their elation? Two answers can be given:

The first is that their optimism is premature and their confidence about the future unfounded. It is easy to believe that everything is possible in the absence of experience with the real world, as is the case with emerging adults, so says one view. This perspective on youthful optimism would predict that emerging adults are in for a rude awakening once they commit themselves to real life at age thirty. Until then they are too young for their views and values to be given a serious hearing.

On the other hand, the emerging adults of today are the adults of tomorrow. In less than two decades they will be the ones calling the shots so it might be wise to listen to what they have to say. Today's emerging adults are perhaps the first generation in history that is not beholden to a past and for whom the future is in every sense of the word a wide-open adventure.

> They are like the immigrants who came as pioneers to a new land, lacking all knowledge of what demands the new conditions of life would make upon them.

> They are like "unborn child[ren] already conceived but still in the womb.[5]

Each coming generation offers the world a chance for improvement and renewal. Emerging adults are not only busy forming their identity, but in doing so they are also busy shaping the world of tomorrow. And the fact that they take their time doing this also means that they are extra careful not to repeat the mistakes of previous generations. Their willingness for a time to exchange the certainty of knowing for the integrity of questioning deserves a note of appreciation.

10. Emerging adults and their parents

Parents of emerging adults find the views and behaviour of their children more than a bit puzzling and quite different from their lives when they were growing up. "Trying to understand our twenty-something son or daughter," they might say, "is much like immigrating to a strange country. We neither know our children's language nor their customs."[6] On the surface there seems to be a disconnect between the previous generation and the current one.

Yet the relationship between today's emerging adults and their parents is surprisingly close and relatively free from conflict. There is much that these children admire about the life style of their parents, such as their work ethic and their willingness to sacrifice. Their parents also continue to support them financially during their twenties, especially when they cannot fully pay their own way because they are still in school.

At the same time many parents have concerns about their emerging adult children. They want to know whether their children will adopt their values and their life style, accept their worldview, follow in their footsteps and especially when this is going to happen, if ever. In view of the slow pace of emerging adulthood they are impatiently hoping for their sons or daughters to grow up soon and to become like them. Beyond that, it is troubling for many parents to watch their children's lives go in a direction that is quite different from their own. However, it appears that most parents keep these worries to themselves and that they generally give their children a great deal of latitude in shaping their own destiny.

In assessing the validity of the concerns these parents have about their semi-adult children it should be borne in mind that descriptions by one generation of another generation are of necessity always self-involved. The concerns parents have about their emerging adult children are not just based on an objective view of their children's lives. Those concerns are in part determined by the way these parents experience their own lives.

As for the way today's emerging adults view their parents, they may disagree with elements in their parents' life style, but most of them see no need to openly voice their criticisms. They are generally quite tolerant of the difference in outlook on life between them and their parents and they largely have chosen to just quietly go their own way. All this entails, however, that there is very little dialogue between today's emerging adults and their parents about life's most fundamental issues and this in turn adds to the homelessness these twenty-something young people feel.

CHAPTER TWO:

EMERGING ADULTHOOD:

A remix generation in a digital world[7]

As in the chapter before, this chapter contains a series of items characterizing emerging adult life but this time specifically focused on the digital, remix, democratic and collaborative nature of the life style of twenty-something youths.

The influence of digitalized information currently available by means of a wide variety of computing devices is far more pervasive among emerging adults than among any other age group, with the possible exception of teenagers. Emerging adults have whole-heartedly embraced all things digital and are in many ways the more tech savvy generation. This is a major factor distinguishing them from previous generations.

Their enthusiasm for all things digital is evident from their consumption habits. More than any other age group they are in possession of all the necessary digital tools for surfing the net and texting their friends. Typically they are also in hot pursuit of the latest digital communication gadgets such as iPhones and iPads offered on the market. Their enthusiasm further shows in the way they respond to the computerized digital information that they access by means of these tools and gadgets. They have by and large bought into the pull of this type of information and are allowing it to significantly influence the structure and the direction of their everyday lives. In attempting to solve their problems of living they do not turn to books on science, philosophy, or religion for guidance, but to the net for advice. They google their way through life. They spend a large amount of their time surfing the net and texting their findings to one another. They practically live in this virtual world. What may be the reason for this historically new phenomenon?

1. Digital

Emerging young adults were born and grew up immersed in information technology. They are said to be the "most informed generation" of all times. Throughout their young lives they were "bathed in bits and bytes of information". But what is the nature of this "information"?

It is "digital" information, i.e. it is virtual reality rather than (the immediate experience of) everyday reality. What we experience when we access computer information is a certain *form* of information, information that is digitally shaped by the medium that delivers it. It invites us to make a statement of opinion or preference with respect to the specific information that is offered. Digital information is information that is inherently open to evaluation and appropriation as a response.

More concretely, this type of information is like a gigantic dictionary or encyclopedia, which provides knowledge on any conceivable topic. Like an encyclopedia it provides the user with a multitude of largely unverified facts. For that reason it looks more like a compendium of opinions than data, each of which may or may not conflict with other opinions. The sheer volume of digital information requires specific cognitive skills such as skimming, scanning, scrolling, surfing, sorting, categorizing and creatively tinkering with this information. For all these reasons digital information presents the user with a collection of stand alone bits of knowledge, and, because of its fragmented nature, invites one to combine and re-combine these items into ever more innovative configurations. In short, computerized digital information is tailor made for remixing its components into a changeable collage of style and preference. The whole of this activity takes on the quality of a game. In comparison with everyday experience, and regardless of how one attempts to process digital information, it is at best a facsimile of everyday experience. It is hard to escape the sense that this type of knowledge is inherently artificial.

2. Remix

It may seem far fetched to draw a causal connection between the nature of digital information and the behaviour of individuals using it, but consider the following quotation from Wikipedia about Postmodernism, (bearing in mind that emerging adults are post-modern to the core.): Postmodernism represents

> a shift into hyper reality in which simulations have replaced the real. In postmodernity people are inundated with information, technology has become a central focus of many lives, and *our understanding of the real is mediated by simulations of the real.* (emphasis added)[8]

Emerging adults do not just passively absorb this type of information but they actively evaluate it and customize or personalize it to suit their own lives. They typically take individual bits and pieces of what they learn on the net and recombine them into their own constructions of a message for their life. This is paradoxically simultaneously an act of independence on their part with respect to this information and an act of obedience to the demands of this information. The very act of remixing the bits and pieces of what they learn into an organized whole subjectively experienced and produced by the users of digital information may be an act of independence ironically necessitated by the fragmented nature of digitalized information.

The end products of this evaluation and reconstruction remix process are opinions or statements of preference by emerging adults, who then communicate their opinions via the net by means of text messages, blogs or tweets to other emerging adults. These in turn repeat the process for themselves. They evaluate the information, choose and remix elements of it into a construction of their own, etc. As a social process these activities are at least partially governed by the character of the digitalized information, the influence of which is so prevalent among emerging adults.

3. The democratization of culture

What is happening in this process, I think, is nothing less than the democratization of culture, or the ongoing creative innovation of existing art and the seemingly never ending revision of current knowledge. Computer technology has made it possible for emerging adults not only to access an unprecedented wealth of music and film. It also enables them to utilize these ancient and contemporary art forms as material for their own artistic productions. They listen to songs, read the lyrics and watch film clips. But they also cut and paste these elements of existing culture, combine them innovatively into their own creative video (re)productions and post them on YouTube.

In addition and by means of twitter and blogging, they participate with other twenty-something adults in an ongoing and spirited dialogue on a vast array of topics ranging from religion to recreation, fashion styles to food preferences, exercise to environmental concerns. In this debate no one opinion is ever elevated to the level of gospel truth. What matters most to these young people is the free exchange of ideas and the right of each individual to speak and be heard. As with the arts, this development represents a democratization of knowledge.

This historical turn of events delivers the death knell to the notion of single authorship. In a climate where everyone is allowed to be the author or composer of her/his own creation, the idea of an original composer or author who has the sole copyright for his/her production becomes problematic. The debate of the so called "creative commons" about the right of anyone to download existing cultural products free of charge is an example of the current actuality of this issue.

4. Collaboration

In distinction from previous generations emerging adults promote and practice collaboration rather than competition wherever they can. Whether at work, with their friends or in their family, they want their views to be heard and they are most willing to give the views of others a sympathetic hearing. When faced with a problem they tend to consult with others in the conviction that the more people contribute their ideas about solving the problem the better the solution.

Take for example the way they purchase an item for sale. Before they decide to buy it they research this product thoroughly from every possible angle, its price, the reputation of the company which manufactures or sells the desired item, they compare it with alternatives on the market, and they contact the company to see whether it is willing to customize the item to suit their specific need. But having done all that they will not make the purchase without seeking the advice of their peers and they are more likely to buy an item if their friends have already bought it and found it to meet with their satisfaction. Emerging adults are less likely to be influenced by the way a product is advertised and rely most often on their peers for deciding to make the purchase. In this way buying a product is a collaborative process for them.

At work they are eager to contribute their ideas to the running of the company they work for. They are most productive when working together with other employees in groups. They welcome rather than fear the critique of their ideas by other workers and they favour solutions to problems that are the product of collaboration. To them work is best done as teamwork rather than individually. Decision making, they feel should be democratic, done from the bottom up rather than from the top down. This preference often leads to friction with the philosophy of the management in corporations that are hierarchically structured, as most of them tend to be.

They learn best in schools where education is interactive. They get along with parents more easily in egalitarian families where rules of behaviour are the product of discussions in which they have a say.

They have no problem living at home even after they have been away to university, provided they can access the net at will without supervision in the privacy of their own bedroom. Ironically, the Internet enables them to stay in touch with other family members while they are away. But also, because computer technology has created a physical distance in their home between them and their parents and siblings, there is less actual communication happening.

Much of their interaction with their peers occurs on line rather than face to face. With them they share in a community, in which they can be themselves together with others. Within this community communication is world wide and instantaneous. In it tradition and privacy are of lesser value; personal expression, openness and novelty are at a premium. Since they are aiming to inform rather than impress one another the language of discourse is easygoing, colloquial, concrete and about the most mundane events of their lives. The whole of it has the flavour of neighbours talking across the fence with one another at the end of the day. Emerging adults find this virtual reality so much more user friendly than their everyday reality and this may be the primary reason why they spend so much of their time on line.

CHAPTER THREE:

Hipsterism

Hipsters and the practice of irony[9]

One more characteristic of the lifestyle of emerging adults is the ironic nature of their speech and behaviour. Irony has been defined as the incongruity between appearance and reality, or between intention and achievement. One will not often find emerging adults speak unambiguously or behave in a manner that clearly reveals their intention. They cannot afford to. We live in a culture that is saturated by advertising. Wherever we go, someone is trying to sell us a product or a service and the truth or falsehood of what is shown, said or done is incidental to its purpose of trying to sell us something. In such a climate one can no longer say heartfelt, sincere things outright because all genuine utterance will inevitably be stolen and repeated as sound bites in advertising. For this reason I have added a separate section on the life style of hipsters because they best illustrate an ironic way of living.[10]

Hipsters form a relatively small sub-group of emerging young adults in North America. They are worthy of note because they both resemble and deviate from mainstream emerging young adult culture. They may also serve as a comparison group and as another illustration of life as a remix process. Hipsters tend to congregate in major North American cosmopolitan centers that formerly were ethnic neighbourhoods but which, because of gentrification have by and large lost their ethnic character. They can be distinguished from other twenty-something young people by their peculiar fashion, behaviour, interests and attitudes.

1. Fashion

Hipsters can be easily spotted by the way they dress. A hipster is someone who looks like a hipster. Their fashion style is a deliberate pastiche, a hodgepodge, jumble, collage, mash up or melting pot of style items borrowed from surrounding ethnic cultures and from fashion styles that were once popular, but now are no longer *en vogue*. They reject the, in their eyes culturally ignorant, attitudes of mainstream consumers and are often seen wearing vintage and thrift store inspired fashions. Male hipsters dress in tight fitting "skinny" jeans and t-shirts advertising obscure bands or b-movies, covered by flannel shirts or v-neck sweaters, with accessories of painted old school sneakers, thick non-prescription horn-rimmed glasses, truckers hats and big belt buckles, while sporting a conspicuously prominent mustache. Female hipsters tend to wear retro-style dresses and racer back tank tops without bras. In addition, both have a penchant for androgynous hairstyles like messy shag cuts and asymmetric side swiped bangs. Finally, and in spite of misconceptions based on their aesthetic tastes and looks, hipsters tend to be educated, often have university degrees and not infrequently come from relatively well to do middle class families.

2. Behaviour and interests

What probably marks them as much as anything as a visibly identifiable group is their preferred simplified mode of transportation and esoteric tastes. They ride fixed-brake- bikes, (bikes that have no gears or brakes). They drink cheap beer (Pabs, Blue Ribbon, or occasionally, Budweiser), and smoke cigarettes that no one else smokes anymore (Parliament, Lucky Strike or hard to get foreign cigarettes like Galouises). They tend to have elitist tastes in film, music and literature. They enjoy watching indie flicks or foreign films with sub-titles. They listen to indie rock, especially to unknown local start-up bands and they enjoy reading books that no one else reads. They spend much of their time googling for information about these topics and like to talk with fellow hipsters about their knowledge at parties.

3. Attitudes

It will be clear that hipsters are a remix culture *par excellence* in the sense that they love to hunt for tidbits of Internet information and to collect them in an ever-changing hybrid aggregate of lifestyles. Like the behaviour of emerging adults in general hipster culture betrays a Pac-Man mentality. They do not read or look but skim, scan, scroll, and surf. They collect, consume and regurgitate experiences. It will also be clear that the lifestyles they assemble and reassemble are deemed to be esoteric by conventional standards.

4. Hipsters as seen by outsiders

In fact, much of what is written about this way of living describes hipsters in pejorative terms. The reaction of commentators on the hipster lifestyle is overwhelmingly critical even to the point of loathing. What evokes such strong negative emotions on the part of these commentators is that, in their judgment, hipsters contribute nothing new or praise worthy to contemporary culture.

Hipsters are said to have produced nothing original. Their style is entirely made up of elements foraged from other cultural groups, with whom they do not identify in solidarity but from whom they appropriate/cannibalize only bits and pieces indiscriminately. They then combine these elements/symbols/icons of qualitatively different/distinct/disparate styles (working class, counterculture/revolutionary, gay, upper class intellectual cultures) and juxtapose them unchanged into a mashup of their own, thereby reducing these cultural elements to kitsch, i.e. render them irrelevant and meaningless for contemporary living.

Furthermore, they are accused of being snobbish and elitist. They consider their own mashup style of living to be superior to non-hipster mainstream styles. They sneer at Mainstream styles and poke fun at them. Ironically they even go so far as to deride their own life style and poke fun at their tendency to poke fun at other people. So, while reducing non-hipster styles to kitsch, they present their own style of living without conviction, as a joke, as a fashion statement only, wearing it as a costume, parading it on stage as if they are just playing a role in a comedy, rather than expressing their personal individuality. They are in short playing Mr. and Mrs. Dress up to an audience for the effect. They consider themselves to be beyond taking themselves seriously. Or so outsiders tell us.

They pretend that all of this is only a game. They routinely tend to treat serious subjects in a playful, humorous manner. They are especially masters at irony. When asked, they flatly deny that they are hipsters or are living a hipster life style. You can have two hipsters angrily accusing each other of being a hipster! They deny that they are making a statement with their fashion style when it is obvious that they are, and they consistently profess not to be committed to anything when it is clear from the outside that they are very much invested in their style of living. Hipsters pointedly (!) refuse to take a stand on anything or to say anything with a straight face. They refuse to take responsibility for anything. Furthermore, they are working too diligently at showing that they do not care to be believed.

5. Clowns or court jesters?

The whole of this deliberately creates an appearance of inauthenticity, as if nothing matters. All of this raises the suspicion that hipsters actually "protest too much," and I am left with a number of questions.

a) By not even taking themselves serious are they essentially playing the class clown? Clowns of any kind, we all know, are essentially sad individuals who wish to be accepted and respected. But, instead of being taken seriously, judging by what is written about them, the behaviour of these hipster clowns only seems to evoke laughter and derision.

b) Or, have they adopted the role of Court Jester to 21St. Century North American culture? In league with Wikileak, are they aiming to show up the hidden agenda of mainstream America? Are they reminding us of the joke that this culture has become? Contemporary North America has by and large become a mall-centered culture governed by the modern marketing forces of late-capitalism in which the value of everything is reduced to its price and people are treated primarily as consumers. Is the behaviour of hipsters an artfully constructed caricature of this culture to show up this situation?

The chief aim of the hipster lifestyle appears to be to reduce to kitsch anything that is dear to mainstream culture. That culture has by and large become governed by advertising. The nature of advertising is essentially that it lies, or more to the point, the truth or falsehood of its statements is incidental to its purpose of selling us something. Moreover, in mainstream North American (and also European) culture one can no longer say heartfelt, sincere things outright publicly because all genuine utterances inevitably will be stolen and repeated as sound bites or slogans in advertising and in politics.

By way of defense hipsters have taken refuge in irony. Everything about them, the way they act, the way they look and what they say is characterized by double-speak, as if they deliberately aim to outdo advertising. If so, by doing this and more than any other emerging adult age group, they have become poster boys and girls for Post-modernism.

6. Hipster view of hipsters

These are some of the issues that arise when one consults the outsider's view of the hipster lifestyle. But how do hipsters view themselves? On that score I have very little data. What little I have comes from a series of interviews I did recently with members of the hipster colony in the Mission District of San Francisco. These interview data represent their response to the questions I put to them.

When I asked the question: "Who or what is a hipster?" they gave the following answers:
"Hipster" is a general term for many different kinds of young people. It is a term that "the outside" puts on us young people. We don't call ourselves hipsters, but if asked point blank whether we are, we don't mind being called that. "Hipster" is mainly a fashion style statement, (e.g. retro clothes from thrift stores), that depicts a life style marked by irony. Hipsterism is a deeply personal life style, i.e. each of us hipsters follows his/her own individual approach to life, a style of living that cannot be characterized as group behaviour. We do not join groups for social action of any kind. We tend to congregate together with other like-minded young people in groups for support, as here in the Delores Park in Mission. But each of us just wants to be him or herself.

When asked what motivates them to live this hipster life style they did not want to disclose what is inside of them. That belongs to each of us alone, they said. On the other hand, they were willing to state that hipsters are mostly young people who are socially progressive and anti-mainline culture. Furthermore, they stressed that they *are* serious about becoming adults, but they insist on taking time to sort things out before they settle down. They also wanted to lay to rest the myth as if hipster young people are just a bunch of dummies. All young people in the park here, they said, are highly educated, even over educated for the work they are doing. Finally, they think that the reason why older people cannot understand younger people is because of a communication problem that exists between the generations due to age differences. So, they appreciate it very much when an older person takes the time to try to understand them.

7. Hipsters, emerging adults and mainstream North America

When asking how hipsters view themselves what strikes me is how similar they are to emerging young adults in general. In the main, they just want to be themselves, live their own life and at their own pace. As we saw also, like so many other young people they are deeply invested in a remix culture in response to a digital world. But there is one characteristic about their lifestyle that is not found as much among emerging young adults and this factor, I think, explains much of their quirky, ironic, esoteric behaviour.

The distinctiveness of the hipster lifestyle may be found in the answer to the question why they live the way they live. What seems to motivate them, more than anything else I can think of, is their fear of being co-opted by mainstream North American culture. All of the efforts of hipsters appear to be governed by a deeply rooted desire to exclude themselves from that mainstream culture.

What is ironic is that in all their efforts to opt out, they actually resemble mainstream North American culture more than any other contemporary youth group.[11] For, a case can be made that the strength of this culture does not lie in the originality of its ideas nor in its capacity to innovate. Rather, its power derives from its unique ability to forage, digest and package big ideas and novel inventions originating in cultures other than their own. So, like the lifestyle of the hipsters, North American culture does not ever produce anything new but merely remixes elements found elsewhere? If so, then hipster culture is to be located at the centre of Mainstream America rather than at its margins.

8. Irony as a lifestyle: from nothing fits to nothing *should* fit

Hipsters are postmodern to the core. Postmodernism is the worldview that moves from the experience that nothing fits to the prescription that nothing *should* fit. When one starts from the conviction that nothing *should* fit, then trying to identify even pockets of order in an otherwise absurd world or attempting to fit things together that in themselves are absurd is seen as a form of selling out. Irony as a lifestyle is not only a recognition that nothing fits but also a lifestyle that *must* respond to any forms of order, be they philosophies, religions, institutions, organizations, or convictions with critique and disavowal.

CHAPTER FOUR

Intergeneration

Between the generations

In this chapter we will explore how emerging adults and previous generations differ from one another and how they can profitably communicate with one another. Of course, one can argue that there is nothing to explore since people, whether young or old, are first and foremost human beings who all struggle with the same problems of humanity and, as a matter of fact, regularly communicate with one another about these problems.

Furthermore, one can always point to older adults who act like the emerging adults and to emerging adults who act like older adults. So, where does one draw the line? Developmentally speaking, when does a younger generation end and an older generation start? The literature generally pegs the time frame for emerging adulthood between 18 and 30. That would make age 30 the start of the older generation! So, lots of problems exist in defining the precise boundaries of the generations.

Yet, generational differences do exist. Many of the parents of emerging adults find the views and behaviour of their children more than a bit puzzling and quite different from their lives when they were growing up. On the surface then, there seems to be a decided difference, or even a disconnect between the older generations and the younger ones. All this entails that today the generations tend to live along side one another with very little dialogue between them about life's most fundamental issues.

1. Normal Generational differences[12]

There always have been, and always will be differences between older and younger people. These are differences in any culture and at any time of history that normally and necessarily exist between younger and older people because of an educational relationship between the two. In this relationship the young learn the ways of the old but also change the culturally established ways of the old and in this way effect cultural change and renewal.

One generation introduces the next to a given culture by transmitting its experience, its expertise, its competence, and its insight into that culture to the younger generation. Without such an educational, culture-transmitting process from one generation to another, no culture can exist for long. In addition to inculcating the next generation into a given culture, the successful transmission of that culture also entails a transfer of responsibility for that culture. Learning involves more than gaining competence in the ways of the old. Insofar as one is able, the learner is also expected to take responsibility for the ways of the old. The success of the educational process can be gauged in terms of whether or not the behavior of the new generation manifests the ways of the old. From this vantage point learners have rightly learned the right things to the extent that they mimic the behavior of their teachers.

However, in being educated into the ways of the old every new generation also changes the ways of the old more or less drastically. During our period of history in particular, this process of change appears to have accelerated to such an extent that generational differences appear to be taking on the characteristics of a generation chasm. Why in *learning* the ways of the old do the young *change* the ways of the old? Education is more than teaching new dogs old tricks. It does not only change persons but cultures (i.e., commonly accepted ways of doing things) as well. Education offers a culture the opportunity to change itself, to do things in a different way. Next to providing cultural continuity, education is also a process of cultural renewal. In this process it is the learner rather than the teacher who changes culture.

Both individual change and cultural change are products of education. As a result of education learners change themselves to suit existing culture or change existing culture to suit themselves. By means of this process they give their stamp of approval or critique on the culture in which they live.

Cultural renewal can be a positive result of education. The older people become, the more they are inclined to miss-identify the way they do things with the way they ought to do things. After decades of working at constructing a certain way of living, people can become so committed to the way things are done that they can hardly distinguish it any longer from the way things ought to be done. Their way becomes *the* way to be taught and lived.

However, the next generation is not so committed to what is taught. Because the old teach the new generation, it stands on the shoulders of the old and can thus be expected to see farther. But also, because young people are not committed to the old generation's way, they can stand *back* from its culture and see more clearly where the way things are done deviates from the way things ought to be done. Thus, a new generation has the opportunity to be properly critical of the cultural products that are taught. It is the responsibility of each new generation to bend the ways of the old into the right direction. The task of reforming culture to make it conform to what ought to be done is intrinsic to learning.

The faithful exercise of this task can renew a culture. Whether cultural change becomes cultural renewal (in the sense of the Greek New Testament word *kainos*, which means "fresh, improved," rather than the word *neos*, which only means "different from before") depends on whether as a result of learning the learner's actions increase the opportunity for humanitarian functioning in a culture.

2. Differences between emerging adults and their parents of the boomer generation[13]

There are major differences today between emerging adults and their boomer parents that transcend normal differences as a result of education. These differences can become obstacles within intergenerational communication. A description of few of the more obvious differences follows below.

As compared to their parents, emerging adults tend to:

- settle down into marriage and start a family about a decade later
- spend a longer time in school and have more education
- be more invested and proficient in information technology
- be future oriented and have less interest in history
- be collaborative rather than competitive
- be given to indirect/ironic communication styles
- be pluralistic in their outlook on life
- have a tinkering, cut-and paste, remix attitude toward the world
- surf the net rather than read books
- scroll, skim, scan for information
- multitask and range widely rather than focus
- value diversity, dialogue, tolerance, interaction and inclusion
- favour unimpeded personal expression over privacy
- be relationship rather than task oriented
- be committed to virtual, rather than face-to-face communication
- spend much of their time social networking (texting, tweeting, blogging) their peers
- send and read only instantaneous, interactive, and brief communication items, (TL;DR: Too long; Didn't read)
- value personal authenticity and relational transparency in interaction with others
- be progressive and democratic in their outlook on life

- distrust established institutions and persons in power

Perhaps the most fundamental way in which emerging adults differ from their parents is that their lives are by and large characterized by the integrity of questioning rather than by the certainty of knowing. They are voracious researchers. Theirs is a probing generation. They view testing as an authentic place to stand. They like to live on the edge, to try new things, to walk in a space of not knowing, to believe something tentatively for the time being to see where it leads them. They are receptive to otherness, welcoming of diversity, open to dialogue, and willing to change their minds. They believe that all points of view are inevitably subject to revision and doubt that there are many prefabricated truths worthy to live by. To them almost everything is (still) up for grabs.

By way of contrast, their parents have a stake in maintaining that some things must be true no matter what. They feel uncomfortable with so much openness and uncertainty. It has taken them years to craft a credible way of living of their own and they feel that their life style is currently under attack. They secretly want their children to adopt their values and their lifestyle, to accept their worldview and follow in their footsteps but see very little evidence that this is happening. It is troubling for many parents to watch their children's lives go in a direction that is quite different from their own.

However, it appears that most parents keep these worries to themselves and that they generally give their children a great deal of latitude in shaping their own destiny. Moreover, there actually is much that these children admire about the lifestyle of their parents, such as their work ethic and their willingness to sacrifice. Notwithstanding their concerns, their parents also continue to support their children during their twenties, especially when they are still in school.

As for the way today's emerging adults view their parents, they may disagree with elements in their lifestyle, but most of them see no need to openly voice their criticisms. Thus, the relationship between today's emerging adults and their parents is surprisingly close and relatively free from conflict. All this entails, however, that there is little dialogue happening between today's emerging adults and their parents about life's most fundamental issues. The best they can come up with, it seems, is a peaceful co-existence between two solitudes.

It is said that today the lifestyles of the younger and the older generations differ so widely from one another that they might as well be living in different worlds. Yet, as a matter of fact these generations populate the same planet, belong to the same society, live in each other's homes or neighbourhoods and actually are meant to complement each other. How are they to relate to and to communicate with one another?

3. Factors hampering and factors fostering intergenerational communication[14]

What does it take to bring these two worlds into a more relevant contact with one another? In every form of interhuman contact between friends, marriage partners, parents and children and also between the generations, a creative tension exists between identity and relationship, between individuality and communality, between who we are inourselves and what we have in common with others. What we want for ourselves at times runs counter to what we have in common with others.

When this happens and for the sake of a relationship, we are sometimes willing to sacrifice part of our identity, to become like the others want us to be. We are also ready at times to give up our relationship to others in the interest of safeguarding our right to self-expression. What we need to learn is that to be secure in our self-identity we actually need to be related to others and that to be intimately related to others we need to be secure in our identity. We need to master the difficult dance between identity and relationship.

What most often happens instead is that we communicate solely with those who think and feel like we do and we denigrate the views and life style of those who differ from us. We consider our own chosen way of living normal and we label the lifestyle of those with whom we disagree as strange or absurd. We neglect to consider the possibility that there may be more than one kind of normal in the world.

Intergenerationally this form of miscommunication revolves around the notion of "reality". Instead of acknowledging that the emerging adult lifestyle of their children is different from their own but equally valid, parents may tend to label their views and behaviour as unrealistic and immature. The underlying assumption is that once they settle down and become more serious about being adults the choices they will make will also become more realistic, and like the choices their parents have made.

Instead of respecting the views and lifestyle of their parents as different but equally valid as their own, emerging adults may tend to view the way their parents live as unrealistically outdated and out of touch with the world of today. Regardless of the truth content of these views by one generation of the other, such evaluations hamper the process of communication between the generations.

To preserve or restart intergenerational communication a change in attitude is required first of all. This entails the mutual recognition and acceptance by the generations that the experience and outlook on life of the other, while different from one's own, is equally valid and needs to be respected. The generations need the support of each other's *difference*. A society of only younger people or only older people is not a good society.

Furthermore, the key to fostering intergenerational communication lies in *appreciating* each other's otherness. Society is of necessity made up of different generations and age groups. A society of only old people or only young people is neither possible nor desirable. Generational diversity is good for society. Acknowledging and appreciating this fact enhances communication between the generations and it, in turn, strengthens the bonds of society.

4. The importance of mentoring relationships and communities for emerging adults[15]

In my experience the best way to promote intergenerational communication in society is through mentoring relationships. In such relationships an older person cultivates a close friendship relationship with a younger person to the mutual benefit of both. A mentoring relationship is more egalitarian than a parent-child, or a teacher-student relationship. In such relationships both learn from one another and both are changed by the other.

There is a general consensus in the literature that emerging adults benefit greatly from a mentoring relationship with a member of the older generation. A mentorship relationship is one, which provides company for emerging adults, which shows respect and caring towards them, and which supports, challenges and inspires them in a context of ongoing dialogue with them. Older adults in these mentoring relationships relate to emerging adults in such a way that both their strengths and their vulnerabilities are acknowledged.

Mentoring relationships between older and younger people are made possible by the fact that older and younger generations need each other and complement one another. This is evident from parent-child relations and teacher-student relations. Children cannot grow up unless parents nurture them and students don't learn unless teachers teach them. But the converse is also true: parents cannot be parents unless they have children to raise, and teachers cannot teach if there are no students to educate. Generations complement each other and that is an important fact to note when dealing with intergenerational communication.

When enough of these relationships have been established, a society takes on the character of what Daloz-Parks calls a *mentoring community*. Mentoring communities such as families, schools, places of work and churches provide much the same mentoring services to these young people in a communal fashion. The tasks of mentoring communities toward emerging adults, mentioned in the literature are manifold, but they all appear to come down to encouraging them to grow up with foresight and vision. In an ongoing authentic dialogue with them mentoring communities are to show hospitality to their potential of becoming. Older adults in these communities are expected to recognize and honour the strengths of emerging adults but also to challenge them to face their problems. Mentoring communities give emerging adults practical support and a place to belong. Most of all they are expected to anchor the promise of their future by providing them with an inspiration for the long haul. In the main, mentoring communities offer emerging adults security for the time being and a viable hope and vision for the years to come.

Mentoring relationships and communities envelop emerging adults into a network of belonging in which they feel safe to wrestle with the big questions of life and in which they feel free to explore worthy dreams about their future. In these communities they can come to terms with the paradoxical nature of human life, where things are hardly ever as they ought to be and in which they can practice some of the skills they need to function as contributing adults in the society in which they live.

5. Reverse mentoring and reciprocal renegotiation vs. socialization/acculturation[16]

Relationships in mentoring communities, even though they involve the same individuals, differ from parent-child relations and teacher-student relations in that they are more egalitarian and also include some aspects of reverse mentoring in which older adults are mentored by emerging adults.

A common definition of the relationship between members of the older and younger generation is that it is characterized by socialization and acculturation. In this relationship according to this definition, older people like parents and teachers introduce younger people into an existing society or culture. The influence flows in one direction, from older to younger.

One may wonder whether this definition of the relationship is still valid in today's world. In this world parents and teachers are no longer the only ones socializing young people. They are not even the most important socializers. Increasingly, mass media personalities, fashion style trendsetters and recording artists have a much greater impact on the life choices and styles of emerging adults. In addition, the influence of peers via social network technologies is pervasive in their lives. Moreover, the reach of all these influences is worldwide, cross cultural and global in its impact.

In addition, given the fact that we live in an age of rapid social and cultural change, young people are often more aware of the direction in which the world is going than their parents or teachers. All this argues for the proposition that mentorship should be augmented by reverse mentorship. Young people also have things they can teach older people, for instance about the future of information technology.

So, the relationship between the older and the younger generations should be interactive, mutually supportive and mutually influencing. In short, it should be one of ongoing reciprocal renegotiation about the shape of a common culture and society. However, no amount of talking with young people will by itself promote intergenerational concord unless we are willing to include twenty-something young people in the running of the world, either in a leadership, or in an apprenticeship role. My long-standing motto about young people has been: "Don't do anything for them. Give them something to do!"

CHAPTER FIVE:

Emerging Adults and Post-Modernism

1. Distinguishing the influence of development and of history in the lives of emerging adults

It is a longstanding maxim in developmental psychology that you cannot adequately describe the lives of a given generation without taking note of *both* the developmental *and* historical factors influencing their lives.[17] A developmental approach classifies people in terms of the age group to which they belong or in terms of the stage of life in which they are living. School-aged children have experiences that differ from those of middle-aged adults and therefore they behave differently. The life experiences and behaviour of teenagers is quite different from the experiences and behaviour of seniors. In the developmental approach the criteria for distinguishing people from one another are age and stage of life.

Historical factors concern the reality that the experiences and behaviours of a group of people are codetermined by the time in history in which they were born and raised. People who were born and raised during the Great Depression have a clearly discernable different lifestyle from those of the post-war boomers because they grew up under different historical circumstances. The same can be said, of course, for all the other cohorts variously labeled post-boomers, hippies, yuppies, generation X, Y, Z and now the generation of emerging adults.

The fact that the current generation of emerging adults can be defined as a *cohort*, i.e. as an age group born and raised at the same time in history, is a reality very much worth noting. If we were to describe them in purely developmental terms as some commentators are doing, then their behaviour could be seen as an aberration of normal adult behavior. Then parents and other older adults could say: "They are just going through a phase, they are taking their time at it but they will grow out of it when they hit thirty. Sooner or later they will act just like us." However, if their behaviour is also historically determined, then they may exhibit some of the behaviours peculiar to their age group even after they have turned thirty.

2. Emerging adults and (post) modernism I[18]

A cultural shift from the worldview of modernism to the worldview of postmodernism has taken place in the last half century, which is in no small measure responsible for the difference between older adults and the emerging adults of today. Older people and today's emerging adults think and feel from out of different paradigms. (A paradigm, like a worldview, is the way a group of people generally looks at, or thinks, or feels about the world in which they live.) Older adults and emerging adults don't think alike. They process information differently and that may be what makes emerging adults such an enigma to older adults.

Older people tend to think like modernists, emerging adults like post-modernists. For modernists there are such things as facts. For post-modernists there are only opinions. When faced with a problem to be solved or an issue to be settled modernists tend to use the so-called "scientific" method. They start with an unproven opinion, or hypothesis, then they test that hypothesis against "reality" and when that hypothesis proves to be correct, i.e. corresponds to this reality, it no longer is an opinion but a fact. And that then definitively settles the matter. It is the truth.

This approach presupposes that we have a direct, unmediated and error-free access to reality as an objective given outside ourselves against which we can test our hunches. Postmodernists deny that. They say that we only have access to our *interpretation* of that reality. "Reality" is always *constructed* and it is never more than a construct we think up. So, to test an opinion for its truth-value never means more than comparing one opinion with another. Some opinions may indeed be clearer or more profound and therefore have more truth-value than others, but we can never escape the circle of conjecture. As someone recently stated, "Truth can only be spoken of within quotation marks."

Our present world is still very much influenced by modernism but it is haunted by postmodernism's suspicion and critique of science's claim to be the ultimate arbiter of what is or is not true. Post-modernists argue that science itself is based on an unexamined paradigm, and determined by an unproven worldview. They state that in our culture science has unfairly co-opted a place of privilege for itself by proclaiming that its story is the only true one and by relegating all other stories to the realm of fables. In reality (!) science is just one story among many with no more claim to the truth than any other. It is just another story masquerading as *the* story above all other stories. So, for postmodernists it is imperative to *deconstruct,* i.e. to question the validity of any story (or *meta-narrative*) that claims to be the truth.

3. Emerging adults and (post)modernism II

On the issue of facts vs. opinion emerging adults clearly side with the postmodernists. In their lives nothing is true no matter what any more. What they miss in life is a sure-fire way to solve problems that works for everybody. They are faced with the fact (!) that the way they try to solve their problems often differs totally from the way the others they meet in the world try to solve theirs. And, in the absence of objective criteria, who is to say that their way of solving problems is better than that of the others? So, they feel that the best they can do is to decide what is best *for them*, and allow others to do the same for themselves. Their motto seems to be, "You in your small corner and I in mine." Of all the generations in the past the emerging adults seem to be most keenly aware of the plurality and relativity of human opinions. On that point they seem to be indistinguishable from the postmodernists.

It will have become clear, I hope, that emerging adults have an aversion to absolutes and a penchant for tolerance. They are typically tentative about their own opinions, while at the same time fiercely defensive of the right of others to freely voice the truth as they see it. In this they are like the postmodernists who hold similar sentiments. An anecdote may illustrate this characteristic more clearly.

A young friend who is enrolled in a PhD program of studies in Canadian university recently complained to me that she found it so difficult to complete her Masters thesis. She had by now accumulated more than enough information but found it hard to compile it all into one coherent document. I could commiserate with her because I had had similar problems when I was enrolled in a PhD program years ago. When I asked her what she found so hard about that her answer surprised me. She said that in order to complete her thesis she would have to state her opinion in absolute terms, as if it were the only truth. "And that," she said, "would make liars out of all those people who do not agree with my version of the truth." The reason she had trouble completing her Masters thesis was she was reluctant to do this.

This anecdote betrays an ethical concern for others that I have also found in other emerging adults. Quite possibly the reason why they are so uncertain about their own lives is their fear that by being more sure of who they are and what they can do, they disqualify the certainty that others may have about their identity and their capabilities. This concern echoes nearly verbatim postmodernism's concern about meta-narratives.

4. An imperfect history of postmodernism

History teaches us a lot about ourselves. It teaches us that in our present modern and postmodern phase of history there is not a whole lot that is new, not much that has not been already. It also teaches us that modernism and postmodernism are historical phases. It teaches us that, given the constantly changing, ricochet character of Western thought and action, we are most likely to morph into a new post-postmodern phase that is radically different from postmodernism in the not too distant future. Suggestive of this change is the fact that the most popular phrase of the past decade, "whatever!" has now been replaced by the phrase "absolutely!".

By taking the long view, history contextualizes what we find confusing and disturbing today, and provides us with a measure of clarity. However, even an abridged version of the history of Western philosophies, such as that of Copleston, takes more than ten volumes to be told. I plan to recite it in less than ten pages! That is nothing short of insane. Yet I see no other way to argue my thesis that post-modernism is really not much new and is merely a stage in history of Western thought, which, given the ricochet nature of this history, is bound to be followed by its opposite. So, by way of situating emerging adults historically, who are so much influenced by postmodernism, I would like to walk us through this philosophical landscape from the Greeks on up.

In the course of this journey, look for the following themes each of which can be found back as ingredients in either modernism or post-modernism:

> *The overriding theme of the history of Western thought and action is the one of alternating order and disorder, or of an alternating emphasis on the definite and the indefinite. This theme depicts its ricochet character. But there are also other themes evident, themes that are equally relevant for describing the history of post-modernism. Such are the themes of reason versus will and individual freedom and the theme of skeptical thought that attempts to eliminate the input of existing traditions from philosophy. Then there is the theme of self-reflection as the therapeutic sanitation of the soul, as a process of self-clarification, as a consciousness raising activity, or as the process of moving from doubt to clarity. A subsequent theme within the history of western thought and action is the theme of human thinking as active rather than reactive, the theme that*

human thought and action are always up to something, closely followed by the theme of reality being a construction of human thought. Of particular relevance for the history of postmodernism is the theme that history is the process of human self-creation, that human thought is historically and culturally situated, and that, therefore, any view of the world it constructs is relative to its time and place in history. This is the theme that human life is a never-ending project of change and cultural renewal. Finally, there is the theme that the best of human understanding is always critical of positivistic science and that it empathically forms the basis of interhuman relationships.

Echoes of each of these themes can be detected in either modernism or postmodernism, which underscores the fact that no new movement can ever escape its place in history.

a. Philosophies of Ancient Greece

The history of Greek philosophy and all the stages of the history of Western Civilization that follow is a form of ricochet history. It skips from chaos to order from clarity to confusion, from the definite to the indefinite, or as Hegel had it, thesis begets antithesis and back again.

It starts with such mythological thinkers as Homer, Hesiod, and Orpheus who explained the being and becoming of the world and everything in it as the result of the actions of the gods. Among the cultures of their time this was not an uncommon way of explaining why everything that exists is the way it is.

But for the Pre-Socratics who came after these mythologists this was a very unsatisfactory way of looking at the world. For one thing, those gods who were said to have caused the world to be were totally unreliable. They would do one thing one time and for no reason at all do something entirely different another time. So, this mythological worldview completely lacked predictability. Moreover, because Hesiod taught that the gods also had come into being, caused by some other, unknown entity, mythological thinking involved Greek thought in infinite regression. It lacked a starting point.[19]

Mythological thinking was far too fuzzy, far too indefinite for the Pre-Socratic Greeks. So, starting with Thales they formulated a worldview in which the origin of the world was to be found in this world itself. The things of the visible world we inhabit, they said, are the result of (re) combinations of four basic stuffs, fire, air, water and dirt. Every thing in our world can be reduced to a combination of these four substances. They lie underneath the visible world like the subway of a big city. To know these stuffs and how they combine gives a person a definite, predictable, uncomplicated worldview.[20] This view of the cosmos helped Hypocrates, the father of medicine, to make his medical diagnoses in terms of four humors of the body. It also helped Galen much later to construct his four-factor, two-dimensional personality theory, which theory even more recent psychological luminaries as Wundt and Eysenck still found useful.

The Greek Sophists who came after the Pre-Socratics tried to live their lives as if only those four stuffs were important. But they found this Pre-Socratic world-and-life view much too definite and confining. The empirical reality they daily experienced was far too colourful, variegated and complicated to be explained by some four-factor worldview. So the Sophists rejected this pattern for living out of hand as so much intellectualistic speculation. They emphasized the individuality of things and instead of logical thinking they promoted non-logical, more aesthetic ways of relating to the world. They valued the *in*definiteness and *un*predictability of human life.[21]

After them Plato and Aristotle sought to include both the definite orderliness and the changeable, indefinite unpredictability of the world we live in into their magnificent cosmological, anthropological and epistemological thought constructions. Plato did it by constructing two worlds, a world of ideal forms, or eternal verities, a world where all is predictable and nothing ever changes, a world accessible by thinking alone. And he constructed a more familiar world of matter, accessible via sense perception, a much more colourful world, but a world where nothing is predictable or lasting, where everything you believe depends on your point of view. Two worlds, the one definite, orderly and predictable, the other, not.[22]

For Aristotle the relation between the definite and the indefinite in the world was governed by the distinction between form and matter. All things, he taught, consist of indefinite, potential matter that strives to become definite, actual form. The acorn is destined to become an oak tree, marble can become a statue, wood a chair or a table.[23]

b. Hellenistic Philosophy

It may be that Plato and Aristotle made room in their thought constructions for both order *and* chaos, but it is clear that for them order eventually gains the upper hand. The definite triumphs over the indefinite. That was not what the Hellenistic Greeks who came after Aristotle empirically experienced in their world. The world of their time was in an uproar. It was a world of war, famine and sickness. So, they lost faith in the logically constructed world systems of these intellectual giants. Instead they opted for a more chaotic view of reality that was in keeping with their world of experience and they advocated a lifestyle of *ataraxia* or the *escape* from this chaotic reality. Thus, in the history of Greek thought the definite and the indefinite alternated in taking center stage.[24]

The relation between the definite and the indefinite has become a major theme in the history of Western thought and action subsequent to the Greeks.

c. Philosophies of the Middle Ages and the Impact of Christianity

Probably the most shocking event after the Greeks in the history of Western thought was the entrance of Christianity into the Hellenistic world at the beginning of the Middle Ages. This event was revolutionary because the Greek Mind and Hebraic-Christian Mind are quite different and in many ways opposed to one another. Greek thinking tends to be abstract. Hebraic-Christian thought is essentially concrete. To the Greek Mind the relation between the Divine and the world, including its relation to human beings, is one of reason, for Christians the relation is one of love. But the most fundamental difference between these two mindsets relates to the direction they want human life to go. For the Hellenistic Greeks of that time, more specifically for the Neo-Platonist Plotinus, the meaning of human life was to *escape* this evil world, to deny that one has a body and, by means of a life of asceticism and intellectual contemplation, to reach for contact and union with the Divine, who was believed to be eternally beyond this world. Someone described Plotinus as a man who was ashamed of having a body. The meaning of life for him, and in that he personified the Hellenistic Greek Mind was literally out of this world, and *extra*-ordinary.[25]

The contrast between this view and the central teaching of the Christian religion is huge. The meaning of the Christian life is entirely defined by the incarnation of the Divine. It is in essence the idea that God becomes down-to-earth. By entering this world God comes down to us and lives in the neighbourhood, dwells with us there, and like us, takes on a body of flesh, blood and bones, and in effect becomes matter. In this way the central theme of Christianity asserted the fact that meaning is to be found in the everyday events of our ordinary lives. The direction of the Greek Mind was upward to God; the direction of the Christian Mind was downward to us. For the Greeks union with God was to be *achieved* by walking the difficult uphill life path of denial. Christians view union with God as a free gift of grace. To get it takes no effort. All you have to do is accept and *receive* it.

I believe that this teaching about the importance of ordinary life, which must be received as a free gift of grace is the essence of the Christian religion. However, historically grown medieval Christianity was anything but the ideal picture of the Christian life I have just sketched. The Church Fathers who were leaders of the early Church after the apostles had died were faced with two opposing sources of inspiration, Greek Hellenism and Hebraic Christianity. To harmonize these two ways of living they formed a synthesis between Neo-Platonism and the Christian religion. This had as an effect that the lives of the members of the Church during the Middle Ages became more Neo-Platonic than Christian. Neo-Platonism turned medieval Christianity into a world-avoiding religion, in which the most important activity of life was the intellectual contemplation of the Divine, who was principally hidden from view. It promoted a way of living that had as its aim to come to know that hidden God *in our minds.* The observable, evident things of this world were said to obstruct this process. (*The idea of*) God became the most important reality in life. Everything else had to fall into place around it.[26]

This sentiment was evident in attempts by scholars like Anshelm and Aquinas to logically prove the existence of God. The aim of this highly intellectualistic exercise was to provide a rational ground for belief in the Christian God. But paradoxically, it had as a result that it made this God subject to logical necessity. It restricted the freedom of God. In this frame of mind God could only do what was logically possible. This way of thinking about God produced such logically unsolvable problems, earnestly debated by the medievals, as whether God can create a stone so big that he Himself can't lift it.[27] To safeguard the freedom of God against the onslaught of this abstract theological type of reasoning another medieval scholar, Duns Scotus by name, formulated his philosophy of *Voluntarism,* in which he placed the *will* of God above the *reason* of God. He argued that God is free to do as he pleases, whether this makes logical sense or not. By implication, this doctrine of free will as transcending reason soon became applied to human beings as well by scholars of the Renaissance movement. Human beings are essentially free, they taught. The thinking of human beings is governed by the choices they make. To understand human beings one must know what motivates them, one must understand their *internal frame of reference.*

It would be easy to view this debate about the priority of will versus reason between Anshelm and Aquinas on the one hand and Scotus on the other as yet another instance of the problem of the relation between the definite and the indefinite. And, of course, it was that. But I think that there was something much richer and more profound going on in this debate. I think this debate actually represented a clash between the Greek Mind and the Hebraic-Christian Mind. In any case, the debate points to the fact that there are two main sources of inspiration operative in the history of Western thought.

In my view the idea of will is not of Greek origin but has Hebraic-Christian roots. When Scotus formulated his philosophy of Voluntarism he appealed to Augustine, who lived some nine hundred years earlier and who is often called the last Greek thinker and the first Christian thinker. Augustine taught that the relation of God to the world and to humanity is one of love. Scotus taught that the free will of God, while it supersedes the bound of reason, is not arbitrary because it is rooted in love. It is impossible to love on command. To love someone entails that you have freely chosen for that person. Love also implies an awareness of the uniqueness of the other. What we love frequently is the otherness of others, is the fact that they possess qualities that we lack. This kind of love is also spontaneous, unpremeditated, uncalculating and not thought through, or non-reasoning. Love is blind, we say.

All of these characteristics we find in the Voluntarism of Scotus. Historically these values of love, will, individuality, spontaneity and intuition prompted Pascal, some four hundred years after Scotus to exclaim that "the heart has reasons of which reason knows nothing." The debate between Anshelm and Aquinas on the one hand and Scotus on the other had as its result for the history of Western thought that in many ways reason and will came to be seen as each other's opposites.[28]

d. Philosophies of the Modern Period: Empiricism-Sensationalism and Rationalism-Romanticism

Following the Middle Ages two intellectual movements dominate the. Modern period in the history of Western thought. The one is British Empiricism, which for our purposes also incorporates French Sensationalism. The other is Continental Rationalism and its rebellious offspring, Romanticism. Both these movements of the Modern period differed markedly from intellectual movements of the Middle Ages. Middle Age philosophers all taught that in addition to the capacity to think and to observe, human beings need the help of tradition to be able to come to know what is true.

For the Christian thinkers that involved the authority of the bible or of Church doctrine. For Renaissance scholars the process of coming to know truth required the authority of the Greek and Latin Classics as a necessary condition. By contrast philosophers of the Modern period held that human beings have within themselves the capacity to perfect themselves without the need for outside input, provided they think straight and also, as in the case of Empiricism, provided they observe correctly. Thus, Modern philosophy was a philosophy that attempted to eliminate the input of tradition from philosophy and had as its other aim the self-perfectibility of human beings.[29]

e. Continental Rationalism

The object of this brief history of Western philosophy is to describe the historical precedents of postmodernism. In the interest of limiting space, I will skip a description of Empiricism-Sensationalism and concentrate on the historical strand of Continental Rationalism, since this strand best illustrates many of the themes found in postmodernism.

Continental Rationalism focused its attention more on the acquisition of self-knowledge than British Empiricism and French Sensationalism in which the focus was more on our knowledge of the world. The belief of Continental Rationalism was that individual human beings could perfect themselves through self-reflection.

The adherents to Continental Rationalism, like Descartes, Leibniz, Wolff and Kant had a number of characteristics in common. They all thought of the activity of the mind as a form of therapy. Thinking for them was a process of internal housecleaning. They viewed philosophy as the "sanitation of the soul". For them the process of coming to know oneself was a process of "self-clarification". The term we would use today is "consciousness raising". The other aspect of coming to know yourself in their view was that of "unifying plurality", i.e. of systematizing or "whole making". Today we might call that the "integration of experience". All of this is possible, so said these Rationalists, because human beings have the capacity to infallibly "represent" reality as it is, i.e. the ability to "reason", or the capacity of "right thinking". Consequently, they also saw this reasoning *process* as a path of *progress*. They held that the inevitable result of this reasoning activity, if people chose to engage in it, would be self-improvement. Via this activity mankind would be able to eradicate the errors of the past. The path to self-knowledge was a path of liberation, of emancipation. This aspect of emancipation through consciousness raising became much later in history the centerpiece of the philosophy of Marxism and of Psychoanalysis. But it had its origin in Continental Rationalism.

Two things must be added to make the initial picture of Continental Rationalism complete. The first is that in its view the mind is always active rather than reactive. It is not informed by reality, but constructive of reality. The second is that this process of coming to know oneself occurs entirely within the individual who does the reasoning. This therapeutic-emancipatory-soul sanitizing-error eradicating process occurs *within* the person. Contrary to what the Empiricists taught, this process requires no external impetus to get started, nor is there an external criterion for judging whether the process is on the right track. The process is spontaneous and self-correcting.[30]

According to Descartes this self-reflecting process moves an individual from a state of doubt to one of certainty. At the start of this process there is much darkness about the answer to the question one is entertaining. But as the process proceeds, it gains more and more clarity. The solution to the problem one poses becomes more and more *evident*. Finally, the answer becomes so *self-evident* that it is impossible to doubt its validity. The certainty one sought after has been achieved.[31]

Leibniz, who came after Descartes in time, emphasized the fact that this activity of clarification is a process of self-perfection. By means of this thought process we actualize our potentials and integrate parts of ourselves into a unified personal whole. Leibniz called this process "perception". Perception is a process of integration, which at the same time is a consciousness raising process. It makes conscious what is *below* consciousness. With Leibniz, and perhaps for the first time in the history of Western thought, the insight breaks through of a sub-conscious. Leibniz again perhaps for the first time in history, stressed the idea that reality is essentially dynamic and perpetually growing. The process of perception is a naturally ongoing, spontaneous growing process in all of us. It may in some way be evoked, or even elicited from the outside, but it is never caused *by* the outside.[32]

The idea that human beings are active rather than reactive vis-à-vis experienced reality is a theme that is continued by both Wolff and Kant. According to Wolff the mind has the ability to represent reality, to hold it before itself so to speak and by representing reality to organize it into a structured whole. In the same vein Kant proposed that the mind immediately orders incoming experience by means of a series of innate categories. Fichte, who started the philosophical school of Idealism after Kant, took this idea that human beings order their experience one step further and proclaimed that reality is a *construction* of the human ego.[33] This theme of the constructive nature of human experience became prominent in later periods of European philosophy.

Thus far my brief description of Modern philosophies. In many ways these philosophies of the Modern period represented a revival of Greek thought with its emphasis on the importance of reason and intellectual pursuits. But they were much more than a repetition of the Greek Mind. The idea that reason occurs principally internal to the minds of individuals and is constructive of reality would have been foreign to the philosophers of Ancient Greece, most of whom subscribed to some form of universalism and realism. The philosophies of the Modern period clearly betrayed the influence of late medieval thought, particularly that of the Renaissance philosophers with their emphasis on free will and the uniqueness of individual minds.

f. Romanticism

That influence is even more pronounced in the thought world of the Romanticists, who followed the Continental Rationalists in time and who were critical of their intellectualism. To introduce the input of Romanticism into the history of Western thought we must go all the way back to Duns Scotus' Voluntarism. The reader will recall that Scotus posited the will as an alternative to reason and logic. Recall further that this notion of will was rooted in love. This love connection between will and love is important for understanding Pascal and also for understanding Romanticism. The motivation behind the views of Pascal and the Romanticists was a desire to stress the importance of caring for human life and human relationships. They reacted negatively to the exclusive emphasis on reason and logic during the Modern period by both the British Empiricists and Continental Rationalists. This one-sided emphasis, in their view, had created a world that was cold and uncaring.[34]

Pascal, for example, who was a forerunner of Romanticism, stressed the importance of the heart as an alternative to reason in the pursuit of self-knowledge. His notion of the heart was deliberately ambiguous. It had many meanings. It could mean the seat, or the instrument of love, of will, of freedom, of spontaneity or of feeling and intuition. The meaning most appropriate for the heart as an alternative to reason and logic was probably the meaning of *intuition*.[35] There are things, which can be known by means of logic, but there are also things that can only be known by heart, intuitively. This form of knowing is an immediate, pre-logical, pre-reflective, spontaneous grasping of the truth of a thing. It depends more on feeling than on logic. For instance in contrast to Descartes who said, "I think, *therefore* I am", Herder, one of the founders of Romanticism said, "I feel, I am!" There is no need in his view for a "therefore". For him the knowledge of his existence was immediate.[36]

One unfortunate by-product of the exclusive emphasis on reason by both the Empiricists and the Rationalists was that they saw themselves as the pinnacle of social and cultural development. They viewed their time as the ultimate age of Enlightenment. Thus, they did not value history as the study of past events since they considered past civilizations inferior to their own. Nor did they think much of cultures other than their own culture of Enlightenment. As proof of their superiority they cited the scientific discoveries their culture had made in the physical sciences and elsewhere.

The Romanticist who most strongly and effectively opposed the devaluation of history and culture by these Enlightenment philosophers was Vico. He began his opposition by stating that our knowledge of physical nature is inferior, and second-hand compared to our knowledge of society and of history. He used a criterion of knowledge used regularly during the Middle Ages, which stated that one couldn't really know something unless one has made it. God made the world of physical nature, said Vico, so only God really knows the natural world. To human beings, the physical world is given only as "brute fact". We can only observe it "from the outside in". However, we see our own lives "from the inside out", and via sympathetic understanding, or empathy we understand the lives of women and men in other cultures and other historical times as well. Therefore, history is the greatest science. History is the study of the process of human self-creation. Human life is a project. Human beings make themselves through history. History is a *Geisteswissenschaft*, as Dilthey was to call it later, literally a "science of the human spirit", a "social" science rather than a natural science. The distinction between the "natural" and the "social" sciences started with Vico.[37]

The upshot of this development was that during the Nineteenth Century a group of scholars who studied the "process of human self-creation" and who were disturbed by the inroads that Positivistic research methods were making into the human sciences began to argue that these human sciences needed their own method of investigation. They considered the method of the natural sciences, of experimentation and statistical analysis, which this Positivism, this grandchild of Empiricism and Sensationalism, was promoting, to be completely unsuited for the study of human experience.

g. Anti-Positivism

These Anti-Positivists were opposed to treating the human sciences as if it were identical to the natural sciences like physics and chemistry. They argued that an experimental approach, to psychology for example, which views the human mind as one physical system among many, fails to deal adequately with the higher functions of the mind like thought, judgment and valuation. It also ignores completely other equally important psychological functions such as feelings, affects, emotion and motivation. So, a natural scientific, experimental approach, they argued, in fact excludes from the purview of psychology the very essence of human experience.

According to the Anti-Positivists reality as experienced by human beings is of an entirely different kind than physical reality. It is subjective, rather than objective experience. It deals with experience that is always connected to an individual subject, or to an "I", or a mind, or some kind of personality structure. For one thing, human experience always presents itself to us as an organized, integrated structural whole. The elements of this experience can only be understood in terms of that whole, as manifestations of this holistic experience. For another, the experience of one individual differs fundamentally from that of another, so that a general theory of human experience is an impossibility. For this reason an Anti-Positivistic approach to the study of human experience generated typologies rather than theories. Furthermore, according to the Anti-Positivists the mind, which is the subject pole of human experience, is always active. It *generates* experience. The structure of the mind is *intentional,* teleological or goal-directed and *dynamic.* It is a structure of motives, purposes, ideals and goals. The human person who does the experiencing is always up to something.

Finally, a natural scientific, experimental approach to the study of human experience is in the nature of the case compelled to view that experience as a mechanism of causal relations, the elements of which are entirely determined by external forces. Thus, it is unable to deal with what are possibly the most essential characteristics of subjective human experience such as spontaneity, choice, creativity, imagination, meaning and value.[38]

h. Verstehen

The Anti-Positivists argued that the aim of the human sciences is not to experiment with human experience but to *understand* it. In order to describe what the Anti-Positivists meant by "understanding" I will introduce the technical term *Verstehen*, and unpack the various meanings this term acquired in the development of Anti-Positivistic thought. Johann Gustav Droysen was the first to coin the term in 1858 when he contrasted *Verstehen* (understanding) with *Erklaren* (explanation).[39] For him these were two different approaches to two different kinds of knowledge, based on Kant's distinction between practical reason and theoretical reason.

Verstehen first of all has the meaning which we already find with Descartes in Continental Rationalism, namely that of the "self clarification of the mind". Another meaning of Verstehen is the one used by Dilthey, (1833-1911). His use of the term was probably the most influential in Anti-Positivism and is similar to the term *hermeneutic method* in biblical or literary interpretation. As used in the human sciences it views human experience as a text, as a narrative, the meaning of which needs to be expounded. This means that the elements of human experience can only be understood or interpreted correctly in terms of the whole of human experience. Human experience, or "the life of the soul" as Dilthey quotes Thomas Reid to say, "is not composed of parts…but is always and immediately an integrated whole."[40]

Yet another meaning of Verstehen is based on the fact that human experience is always individually different. This meaning refers to Wilhelm Windelband's distinction between a *nomothetic* approach to the study of human experience and an *idiographic* method.[41] The nomothetic approach aims to formulate general theories about human experience that are applicable to all human beings. The idiographic method is more typological and attempts to formulate personality descriptions of individual persons in an effort to clarify their unique way of experiencing the world. By extension, what the experimental approach describes as quantitative differences between people in the method of Verstehen are viewed as really qualitative differences. From the point of view of *idiography* human beings differ radically rather than by degree. They are incomparably unique.[42]

When one adopts "Verstehen" rather than "Erklaren" as a research method in the human sciences, one essentially attempts to understand what makes people tick. Specifically, to understand a person's subjective experience one must discover the reasons for, or the motives behind that experience. Sensations and thoughts are viewed as the products of needs and drives rather than the results of the impact of external stimuli. We see what we need to see and think what we want to think. To understand subjective human experience means to look for the activity of the will, the emotions, the affects and the drives that determine our experience. It means that we identify a person's personality, which determines the manner in which he experiences the world. Dilthey stated that to understand someone's experience in the sense of Verstehen one must penetrate his spirit down to his structure of choices, purposes and ideals, values and meanings. The essence of understanding (Verstehen) a person's experience (Erlebniss) is to empathize with (Nacherleben, literally "to experience along with") that person's experience.[43] The end product of such an exercise is that one can truthfully say, " Now I know why this person looks at the world the way she does, thinks the way she thinks, and acts the way she acts."

i. Concluding comments

When we look back into the history of Western thought we can make the following concluding observations. First off, all great Western thinkers accounted for both order *and* chaos, for both the definite and the indefinite in human experience. In modernism the definite reigns supreme, in postmodernism the indefinite. All great Western thinkers also attempted to account for themes from both the Greek Mind and the Hebraic-Christian Mind. Many of these themes are found in postmodernism.

Yet another way of telling the story of the history of Western thought and action is what happens to thinking and logic over time in relation to reality. During the time of Classical Greek philosophy thinking as Reason was seen as the only gateway to ultimate reality. It was the supreme lawgiver. You turned to it for advice on what was real in your life. But already during the time of Hellenistic philosophy, and in fact throughout much of the Middle Ages, thinking became the tool for *escaping from* reality into some extraterrestrial, otherworldly realm.

The philosophies of the Modern period were decidedly this-worldly and critical of the otherworldly focus of traditional Hellenistic and Medieval philosophy. In that sense they were reminiscent of the critique of the mythologists by the Pre-Socratics that preceded them in Greek thought. Moreover, in Continental Rationalism thinking was no longer viewed as the gateway to an eternally, externally existing, objective Reality, as the Greeks had thought, but became an activity *internal to* the human mind. Literally, this view holds that there is no reality outside of thinking that human beings can access or need to reckon with. Thinking is all there is! In fact, thinking actively *constructs* reality.

Yet a little later reality becomes the product of *unique individual human minds*, a view that prompts Carl Rogers, the founder of Person-Centered Therapy, to state his belief centuries later that there are as many realities as there are individual human beings. This turn to the subject, (can we say *escape into* the human subject?) also entails yet a little later that thinking now no longer is seen as the master over one's feelings, urges and passions, but rather their servant. We think what we wish, or fear to think. The dethroning of thinking as Reason is complete when the view takes hold that thinking is thoroughly bound to a given cultural and historical place and time. This puts to death the notion that thinking can ever access a truth that transcends one's time and place in history. Truth is local and can only be spoken of within quotation marks. With that we have arrived at a central thesis of postmodernism.

However, this rendition of the history of Western thought and action is altogether too pessimistic to be left to stand alone. This history can also be told starting with the entrance of Christianity into the Hellenistic world at the beginning of the Middle Ages as the triumph of immediate experience. (It should noted that this *was not* the way the medieval Christians *practiced* their Christianity). This Hebraic-Christian strain in the history of Western thought and action is initially critical of the abstract character of Greek thought and consistently provides a concrete alternative to it by insisting that the relation of the Divine to the world is one of love and passion rather than Reason and logic. This emphasis on the primacy of feeling rather than thinking is further elaborated by Duns Scotus' insight that "will triumphs over logic", by the doctrine of the individuality and inherent freedom of human beings by Renaissance thinkers, by Pascal's insistence that the heart is wiser than reason and by the importance of passion in human life propagated by the Romantics. It comes to its full expression in the notion of understanding (Verstehen) and empathy, rather than logic and experimentation as the way human beings are to relate to themselves, to other human beings, and to the world, concepts dear to anti-positivistic thinkers.

The outcome of this historical development ultimately is the realization that life in all its variegated colour is bigger than thought and *informs* thought. Life does not allow itself to be boxed in by theoretical constructs, however ingenuously they are formulated. With that we have arrived at the postmodern positive appreciation of the fundamental diversity of human experience. It holds that there is fortunately more than one kind of normal in the world. This insight is eminently suited to the global world of today.

Chapter Six:

Personal Postscript

What if the older generation were to listen to the younger generation?

The thesis of this book is that there exists a profound disconnect between the younger and older generations as currently constituted. This makes genuine communication between the generations difficult, if not impossible. The generations are literally worlds apart. The experiential world of younger people is complex, fast changing, global, indefinite and wide open to the future. They are typically tentative about their own opinions, while at the same time fiercely defensive of the right of others to freely voice the truth as they see it. In this they are like the postmodernists who hold similar sentiments.

Perhaps the most fundamental way in which emerging adults differ from their parents is that their lives are by and large characterized by the integrity of questioning rather than by the certainty of knowing. They are voracious researchers. Theirs is a probing generation. They view testing as an authentic place to stand. They like to live on the edge, to try new things, to walk in a space of not knowing, to believe something tentatively for the time being to see where it leads them. They are receptive of otherness, welcoming of diversity, open to dialogue, and willing to change their minds. They believe that all points of view are inevitably subject to revision and they doubt that there are many prefabricated truths worthy to live by. To them almost everything is (still) up for grabs.

From the point of view of the older generation all of the above are negative qualities because they disturb the status quo. But, what if the older generation decided to listen to the younger generation? What would happen?

Few of us today would realistically argue that we live in the best of all possible worlds. The outlook on economic, ecological and civic renewal is bleak and no one in the know today offers a credible vision on how to fix our dilemma. In the words of Arthur Zajonk: " The old forms rattle and the new delay to appear." All this calls for an extended period of fundamental self-reflection. This, in my view, is what young people everywhere are doing. And they ought to be commended for taking their time doing it.

The manner in which they reflect on the state of their soul and on the state of their world is also noteworthy and, perhaps, worthy of imitation. It features a kind of *communal identity exploration*. The central questions for emerging adults remain: *Who am I? Why am I here and where am I going? What can I do, and whom can I love?* But these questions do not represent a lonely search for self-identity. They are embedded in a communal context of dialogue. The questions are peer reviewed. They form the meat of what young people talk about with one another.

Aided by an array of social networking tools emerging adults are engaged in constructing a gigantic, worldwide simulation, a free floating model of what reality could be, might be, a *virtual reality*. The activity occurs on line, via facebook, twitter and blogging, through texting, or brief spoken messages on mobile phones. The entries on facebook are illustrative of this activity. In them young people typically alert their friends to videos they found on the net that made them laugh, smile, cry or admire its creativity. They may pass on articles or statements they read that express their sentiments exactly, or they may offer important information to their peers about the environment, health, finances or politics, which they feel that everyone should know.

These online messages are never passed on as stand alone bits of information. They are always accompanied by commentary. Through them emerging adults inform one another of their opinions and preferences. By means of these messages they tell each other what they consider valuable, important and worthy of review. They are forms of self-expression. Via this exchange of opinions emerging adult get to know one another personally - on line. They are busy building a *virtual community,* in which everyone is allowed to be him, or herself.

This exchange of online opinions and preferences has an as if/what if quality about it. It has the character of a (video?) game. Through it emerging adults take a stab at (play) acting out their future. In the exchange the drama is as important as the information. The exchange is designed to make people laugh or cry, or express anger. At times the exchange is a deliberate attempt at ridicule. Emerging adults have a fine nose for pomposity and hypocrisy, and they are generally critical of it. They also know how to get their point across by merely hinting at it.

One has to admire the enormous creativity of their thoughts, words and actions. They are keenly aware of the value of images and sound bites as icons, as things that stand for something else. They know how to turn a phrase and how to tell a joke. But all this is in the service of some serious business. What they are about is decidedly no joke. In their own non-violent way they are out to change the world. We see this in the mass Arab Spring demonstrations in the Middle East and in the actions of the Occupy Wall Street movement. I think that, perhaps, my son David said it best, when he said that, " young people everywhere are renegotiating their contract with authority."

The dialogue of young people is collaborative rather than combative. They value the critique of their peers and they learn from them. It is also democratic and inclusive, open to all young people all over the world, irrespective of differences in race, religion and culture. However, as currently constituted it excludes the participation of members of the older generations, *if* they insist on views that are non-negotiable. Today's emerging adults are not willing to follow the party line purely on the basis that it happens to be the current status quo. If members of the older generations want to participate in this world wide dialogue they must be open to change. And make no mistake about it, change is coming regardless. Those who cling to the certainty of knowing will be left behind.

On the other hand, dialogue between the generations is possible and even welcomed, yearned for by the youth of today. They have by no means written off the wisdom of members of the older generation. Among other things they value their work ethic and their capacity for sacrifice. The countless discussions I have had with young people who have become my friends through mentorship relationships have demonstrated how rewarding such a dialogue can be for them and for myself. Their insights, most often different from mine, have enriched my life enormously.

Appendix A: A survey of the lives of emerging adults

If you are between 18 and 30, please help me with my research by completing the survey below. The aim of this survey is for me to get to know emerging adults better. Please, feel free to respond to this survey in any way you like.

I would very much like to have this survey be interactive. Of course I would like you to answer the questions I ask. But I would also like you to tell me which of these questions are not important to you or not appropriate to the way you experience your life presently. In addition, I would ask you to write down the questions, which you think a survey like this should ask. I can then include your suggestions into a subsequent version. In this way you are helping me to construct a better survey, one that is focused on getting the most relevant information about your current life experience. In addition to answering the questions, I would also very much like to have you write any additional comments that you may have.

Please send your answers as an attachment to your email message to me at harryvanbelle@hotmail.com Thank you so much!!

Age: _____

Province/city/town in which you live_____

Gender: Female____   Male____

Education: _____

Education of parents _____

Religion_____

Current employment: part time_____, full time_____

          unemployed_____ self-employed ____

other_____

Relationship status: single ____ engaged ____ cohabiting____

married ____separated____ divorced____

Living arrangement: rent alone____ rent with roommates ____

Live with parents____

Other_____

Please provide other data you think I should know:

Please answer any number of the questions below any way you see fit:

1. What are you busy with these days? Please list some of the things that occupy your thinking, your time and your energy. List them in an order of importance to you, so that 1) = most important.

2. Please identify the one thing on the above list that you feel most passionate about. and describe that item in more detail. Also, what are some of the things that bother you the most about your life now and how do you deal with these frustrations?

3. To what extent is the way you experience your life the same or different from the experience of your parents when they were twenty-something? Does this in any way affect your relationship with your parents? If so, how?

4. It is said that persons in your age group are neither adolescents nor adults. Does this also apply to you? If not, what is the case? If so, please describe the feeling of being between these two stages in more detail.

5. It is said that, as compared to the previous generation, the people of your generation have a harder time knowing who

they are and what they can do. It is further said that they spend most of their twenties in search of their identity in the areas of love and work/relationships and career. To what extent do you think does this description apply to you and your friends?

6. Would you say your life right now is simple, stable and predictable or more complex, unstable and unpredictable? Why?

7. To what extent do the social institutions in your world today (government, corporations, banks, schools, marriage, family, church) support you as you live your life? How reliable are they? How much do you have to depend on yourself to make something of your life?

8. It appears that compared to your parents' time you are faced with an overload of choices in your life (vocational, relational, ethical, and religious). To what extent do you relish this abundance of choices and to what extent are you troubled by it?

9. Are your relationships with other people in their twenties, (whether romantic or friendship), currently casual and temporary or more serious and committed? Do you expect this to change as you get older? Do you expect to marry and to start a family? When do you think this might happen?

10. What place does education have in your life today?

11. Please tell me some things about your faith journey from when you were younger to now. What role do religion and spirituality play in your life today?

Appendix B: Emerging Adults in their own Voice:

In this section we let some of the emerging adults whom I have interviewed speak for themselves. Their testimonies show especially how difficult it is for them to make decisions when faced with such an overwhelming abundance of choices in their lives.

(Code: F.= female M. = male Number = age S/M = single or married)

F. 23 S: I do not believe people my age are adolescents. We have too many responsibilities. It is true that we spend more time in search of who we are because there are more options out there.

F. 22 S: I am most passionate about future opportunities that await me. I look forward to beginning a new chapter in my life. I feel as though my parents grew up in a different world than I did. I feel more like an adult than I do as an adolescent. However, sometimes I feel as though I feel stuck between those two stages of development. We are forever asking questions about our identity. At this point in my life I am overwhelmed by the excessive choices available to me. Life seems quite transient. Making choices on matters of some permanence becomes a task that requires a great deal of investment. I hold a very temporary attitude to most of my friendships with my peers. My faith journey is quite murky.

F. 25 M: By the time my mom was my age she already had two children and I was on the way. Our lives were therefore quite different. Choices bring us a lot of freedom and little expectation. With so many decisions to make it is quite easy to make the wrong choice. With all the social networks most relationships are quite shallow and surfaced. Education is very important. It will help improve my knowledge of the job I work.

F. 24 S: My mother was newly married at my age. I get a sense that my parents are waiting for me to figure things out and settle down. They don't understand the appeal of still having flexibility and leaving options open. This causes a gap and creates tension sometimes. I would rather spend time now deciding how I can live best as who I am than struggling my whole life to fit an uncomfortable identity. I might get married, I might not. I may have children, I may not.

F. 22 S: I am most passionate about being there for my friends and I greatly appreciate how my friends are there for me. I see life (only) in the short term (one or two months). I feel frustrated that so much of life is institutionalized and regulated. I think there are many similarities in how I currently experience life to how my parents experienced it. Thus, we are able to communicate freely. Adolescents is way behind me but I also struggle with [not] feeling fully encompassed by the adult world. I am predictably unpredictable. I look forward to not being in constant transition. I often wish I had less choices and that someone would make the big decisions for me. That being said I do embrace the excitement of the unknown and the randomness of choices I am able to make.

F. 31 S: Work has become my life, everything else comes after. I have found that most social institutions do not support the individual. You have only yourself to depend on. I try to be respectful of others faith but right now I have to many questions and anger towards life and spirituality.

F. 22 S: [What] bothers me about the point I am in my life is the amount of pressure there is as I try to juggle work, friends and family. I feel I have a real mix of independence and dependency. I question if people my age are not too casual with their friendships.

F. 22 M: I am mostly frustrated that I do not yet have an idea of what I want to do or how to go about doing it. I definitely feel more mature than a teen. I have way too many options now. Sometimes I wish that I was back in the days when women were expected to stay at home and take care of kids and the household.

F. 20 S: I would like to live with [my boyfriend] for a while prior to getting married. This makes so much sense to me. However, despite that it is OK for me, I often feel disgusted and disappointed in other people who choose to live that way. I feel I am stuck between my parents' values and the values of my generation. I do find financial struggles to be very stressful. I think my parents have trouble understanding my generation, with all our technology need for continual connection with all our friends.

F. 23 S: We are all trying to figure out who we are and plan out of lives right now because soon we will be adults.

F. 20 M: The thing that bothers me about life right now is feeling insecure about job security. I try to deal with this by having the best education and make connections that will help me in the real world. We spend so much time looking for our identity, and relationships and our career. I think this is a huge problem/issue we all deal with. It seems that people either get married earlier or they wait a really long time.

F. 20 S: I feel life is busier and faster paced for me than it was for my parents. We have Internet and cell phones, which makes communication instant, while my parents actually wrote letters home from college. Sometimes I feel that I really don't know who I am, where I am going, or even where I want to be. I want to make something of life, but I don't know what it is yet. I feel rather alienated from institutions (banks and government) a lot of the time. I think my attention span is rather short. I also find the flexibility of truth that seems to be prevalent in our society rather troubling. If we don't know what is true and right then what solid foundation can we hold onto? I want to know. Church attendance is not a measure of spirituality in my book.

F. 20 S: I feel like school is taking too much of my time. I am a very relational person and would love to spend more time with the people who mean the most to me. My parents were raised quite differently (mom conservative, Dad more "wild").

F. 27 S: The pace of life is definitely different from my parents. I go to bed with a cell phone and a Blackberry. I am also in the information age, which means bombardment and more to cram into 24 hours. I cannot turn to my parents for support, especially because I am in the digital era. My life is complex, unstable and unpredictable.

F. 23 S: I know exactly who I am - but the more I live life in our society, the more I realize that I don't belong here. There are times when being so alone, both romantically and otherwise is nearly unbearable.

F. 20 S: My parents didn't go another six years to school when they were 20 years old, in the way I want to make a career, (medical doctor). They also started very young with children. But they support me very well, are proud of me and they understand my choices.

F. 26 M: I am comfortable with who I am and where I've come from, and I have concrete goals for the future. It is my passion to help people, like I myself have been helped in times past.

M. 22 S: I am troubled by the choices previous generations have made, and that is certainly a core influence on the choices I make today. I have no desire to leave this earth in worse off condition than I received it.

M. 20 S: We are told we have the freedom to achieve anything and are expected and demanded to achieve the extraordinary regardless of ability or desire. Spirituality and religion play very little role in my life, simply because I do not feel they provide tangible benefit.

M. 25 S: My life experience is very different than my parents. By my age they already had 2 kids and a house of their own. It has always been up to me to make something of myself and that is the way it should be.

F. 25 S: I have the maturity that removes me from adolescents, but I don't have all the responsibilities of adults as I am still in school working to establish my career. I am constantly debating if I have chosen the right career path, and have in fact changed my route twice.

F. 22 S: It seems that people have more choices so there is greater discrepancy of what people my age decide to do. I do not want to have kids right away, as I want to travel first and establish a career.

F. 30 M: It seems that it takes this age group (emerging adults) a long time to become more adult-like. In some ways it's as though you want to pack in as much "fun" and varied experiences such as traveling while you're in your twenties. I am jaded by the politics and problems that religion seems to bring with it. Overall, I have stripped my faith back to the basics. My spirituality can be expressed in love and service to others.

F. 26 S: I hate feeling like I am not in control!!! I still feel like there are some things I cannot talk about with my parents because I feel like they will "not approve" and it is easier to simply not have those conversations.

F. 27 M: I have always felt that I didn't have enough information to make commitments. Many of my friends and I are of the mindset that you don't know everything and are open to the possibility of change in anything from eating habits to important ideals. You don't know what you don't know. I am in no position to judge anyone's decision and I can live knowing my choices are fine but not the only ones. Just because what I am doing feels right does not make another choice wrong.

F. 22 S: I spend a lot of time thinking about myself, mostly about my future, what I am doing now, what I wish I was doing, what I hope to be doing in the future. How I can make sure that I'm doing what I want to be doing, and how do I even know what I want to be doing. I am constantly realizing that I can do whatever I want, I can be friends with who I want, I can marry or not marry, I can be whoever I want. It is a little overwhelming. I don't have any answers, only questions really. I often wonder when I am going to get my "adult card". Sometimes being between (being an adolescent and an adult) is more like not being a real person. You can't claim either group, and neither of them is going to claim you either. You're kind of a nothing. Being an adult is all about stability, which is something that is incredibly difficult to obtain when you are just trying to find something that you don't hate and are good at.

M. 29 S: I sometimes feel frustrated by how contingent my life story must be: how randomly things occur, thwarting my efforts to make the most of every situation with "optimal" choices.

F. 27 M: I have a Masters degree. I manage 16 people (most of whom twice my age and respect me for what I am capable of and how I treat them). I own a home and I definitely feel like an adult. I am happy where I am. My identity is strong. I am a lot more comfortable with doubting (about ultimate questions) than when I was younger, but that means I don't struggle as much as I used to and wish I would.

F. 24 S: The overload of choices we face today certainly is overwhelming. Moving out of the big city back to the town I grew up in helped immensely. There is a manageable amount of choice here. I'd love to meet a man to fall in love with and I feel that I would be delighted to be a mother and perhaps even a wife. But I am in no immediate hurry. I want to feel completely at peace with myself, to be able to trust my instincts completely before I share the wealth of my experience with a mate and children. And yes, I'm really beginning to find peace in the simple life; in the quiet place within me.

M. 14 S: I am annoyed that I do not have enough friends. It also annoys me that we teens are too old for this and too young for that. It makes life boring. I study, I hang out with friends. I live-- my life is simple.

M. 27 S: Having not yet had a full time job is something which has bothered and frustrated me for some time taking into account the high cost of living in a city (in Kenya). The cost of living when my parents were my age was low because my parents mostly resided in rural areas. Institutions of higher learning often prepare a student for one particular career but in the process one ends up doing something entirely different, which is ridiculous.

M. 24 S: I get more joy out of playing sports than anything else in life and gravitate to people that share this interest. These choices (vocational, relational, ethical and religious) can seem overwhelming and were major headaches for me growing up. While it's great to have the freedom to choose from a virtual limitless pool of possible career paths, when none jumps out at you it's very tough to pursue one. These decisions and choosing "what I want to do with my life" are very stressful and probably the single biggest source of concern in my life.

BIBLIOGRAPHY

Armstrong, A.H. *An Introduction to Ancient Philosophy*. Totowa, N.J: Rowan and Allanheld, 1983.

Berlin, I. *Vico and Herder: Two studies in the History of Ideas*. N.Y: Vintage, 1977.

Copleston, F.C. *A History of Medieval Philosophy*. Notre Dame: U. of Notre Dame Press, 1972.

_____. *A History of Philosophy*. Vol. VI, Westminster: The Newman Press, 1960.

_____. *A History of Philosophy*. Vol. VII, London: Burns and Oates, 1965.

Descartes, R. *Discours de la Methode*. 1637. Text by E. Gilson, Paris, 1939.

Fichte, J.G. *Basis of the Entire Theory of Science*. 1794.

Herman, J. *Trauma and Recovery*. NewYork: Basic Books, 1992.

Kant, I. *Gessamelte Schriften*. Berlin: Prussian Academy of Sciences, 1902-42.

Kirk, G.S. and J.E. Raven *The Pre-Socratic Philosophers*. Cambridge: Cambridge U. Press, 1963.

Kok, J.H. *Patterns of the Western Mind*. Sioux Center, Iowa: Dordt College Press, 1998.

Leibniz, *Monadologie*. 1714, Transl. by H.W. Carr, Los Angeles, 1930.

Lersch, Ph. *Algemene Psychologie*. Translated into Dutch from the German *Aufbau Der Person*. Utrecht: Het Spectrum, 1960.

Muller Freienfels, R. *De Voornaamste Richtingen in de Hedendaagsche Psychologie*. Translated into Dutch by P.H. Ronge, Utrecht: Erven J. Bijleveld, 1938.

Pascal, B. *Pensees*. Ed. by H.F. Stewart, London, 1950.

Polkinghorne, D. *Methodology for the Human Sciences, systems of inquiry*. Albany: State University of New York Press, 1983.

van Rappard, J.F.H. *Psychologie Als Zelfkennis: Het zielsbegrip tussen substantie en structuur in de Duitse rationalistische psychologie van Wolff tot Wundt en Brentano*. Amsterdam: Academische Pers, 1976.

Wolff, *Gessamelte Werke*. 1713, Hildesheim: George Olm Verlag, 1965.

END NOTES

[1] About me, by way of introduction: I am 75 years of age, in reasonably good health, married for 47 years, the father of three children and the grandfather of three grandchildren. For more than a decade now I have been a retired professor of psychology with a lifelong interest in stages of human development. By virtue of my profession I have been interacting with twenty-something young people for nearly 40 years. I like them. They fascinate me. I like being with them. Even today I am in regular email contact with quite a number of them. They have taught me so much over the years, about myself and about themselves! But there is still a great deal that I don't know and they continue to teach and to fascinate me every day.

The descriptions in this book are meant to give a reasonably accurate picture of the lives of these twenty-something people. However, the distance between their age and mine is enormous, nearly half a century! So, at my age I am well aware of the subjectivity of my point of view. The best I can offer is *my perception* of the lives of these young people. I can only tell what they look like from where I am looking. So, far from giving the low down on emerging adulthood my book is intended as an introduction to a discussion between you the reader and myself. I very much look forward to your comments about what I have written.

Most importantly, I would expect the young people about whom I write to correct me when my descriptions of their lives do not match their life experience. When I was still teaching I would regularly tell my students that nothing pleases me more than that years from now, as a result of my teaching, my students would be able to say *with reason*: "Van Belle was wrong!" For that would mean that they see farther than I can because they are standing on my shoulders.

[2] Much of what I write in this part of the book is an extension of a theory of emerging adulthood developed by Jeffrey J. Arnett. He coined the phrase *emerging adulthood,* and with that started an entirely new research tradition focused on young people in their twenties.

94

Arnett, J.J. 2004, *Emerging Adulthood The Winding Road from the Late Teens through the Twenties.* New York: Oxford University Press.

Arnett, J.J. & J.L. Tanner (eds.) 2006, *Emerging Adults in America, Coming of Age in the 21ˢᵗ. Century.* Washington, DC: American Psychological Association.

Other sources consulted were:
Clydesdale, C. 2007 *The First Year Out, Understanding American Teens After High School.* Chicago: University of Chicago Press.

Joiner, R. Bomar, C. & A. Smith 2010 *The Slow Fade.* Colorado Springs: David C. Cook.

Konstam, Varda 2007 *Emerging and young adulthood: multiple perspectives, diverse narratives.* New York: Springer.

Smith, C. & P. Snell 2009 *Souls in Transition, the religious and spiritual lives of emerging adults.* Toronto: Oxford University Press.

Wuthnow, 2007 *After the Baby Boomers.* Princeton: Princeton University Press.

[3] One more way in which they are made to live in between lives

[4] Personal communication

[5] Margaret Mead, 1970 *Culture and Commitment, a Study of the Generation Gap,* p.72 and 88. Garden City, N.Y: Natural History Press.

[6] To my knowledge, Margaret Mead in her book *Culture and Commitment* was the first to describe the generation gap as parents and their children living in different countries. She ascribed this phenomenon to overly rapid historical-cultural change in our society. This powerful metaphor is still relevant for describing the disconnect between today's emerging adults and their parents.

[7] Much of the material in this section is based on a book by Don Tapscott, who has written extensively on the impact of the information technology.

Tapscott, D. 2009 *Grown Up Digital.* Toronto: McGraw-Hill.

For more on the remix culture see:

http://p2pfoundation.net/Remix_Culture, which article on p.1, gives the following definition:

Remix culture describes the way in which youth culture today more visibly orients itself around creating media by extracting component pieces from other people's media creations, then connecting them together to form something new....
    (original source: http://www.lingualgamers.com/thesis)

Also see:
Heath J. & A. Potter 2004 *The Rebel Sell.* Toronto: Harper Perennial.

and

Coupland, D. 2007 *Jpod.* Toronto: Vintage Canada.

[8] This quotation was taken from an article on irony, http://en.wikipedia.org/Postmodern_literature, p.8.

[9] See http://en.wikipedia.org/Postmodern_literature, p. 5 ff. and Prickett S. cited above.

[10] The description of hipsterism draws on a wide variety of sources:

Books:

Laham, Robert 2003, *The Hipster handbook.* Anchor Books.

Greif, M. Ross, K. & D. Torrorici 2010 *What was the Hipster? A Sociological Investigation.* New York: n+1 Foundation.

Articles/blogs on the net:
    Haddow, D. "Hipsters, the Dead End of Western
        Civilization", *Adbusters Magazine*.
    Cracked.com: Articles on Hipsters
    "On Hipsterism": I was a freight train (author unknown)

Video/film:
    Scott Pilgrim vs. the World
    Flight of the Conchords (comedy)

Magazine:
    Vice, founder: Gavin McInnis, called "the Godfather of
    Hipsterdom"

[11] Heath J. & A. Potter 2004 *The Rebel Sell*. Toronto: Harper
    Perennial.

[12] Van Belle, H.A. "Relational Anthropology and Education" in *Pro
    Rege*, a quarterly faculty publication of Dordt College, Sioux
    Center, Fall 1985.

[13] There are numerous articles on differences between emerging
adults and the boomer generation that can be googled. Here is just a
partial list of some of the titles:

    Millenials, A Portrait of Generation Next: Confident, Connected,
        Open to Change
    GenY vs. Boomers: Generational Differences in Communication
    Generation Y
    Professional and Personal Communication Across the
        Generations
    Different Generations have Different Communication Styles and
        Different Tools
    Grandparents: Looking at the Generation Gap
    A Boomer's Guide to Communicating with Gen X and Gen Y
    Changing Communication Between Generations
    Today's generations face new communication gaps

Books on Generational Differences:

Bibby R. W., Russell, S & R. Rolheiser 2009 *The Emerging Millenials,
    how Canada's newest generation is responding to change and choice.*
    Lethbridge, Canada: project Canada Books.

Tapscott, D. 2009 Grown Up Digital. Toronto: McGraw-Hill.

[14] Van Belle, H.A. *Persisting Themata and Changing Paradigms, explorations
    in the history of psychology.* Pp. 6- 8. (Unpublished manuscript.
    For access google *Harry Van Belle*)

[15] Daloz-Parks, S. 2000 *Big Questions, Worthy Dreams.* San Francisco:
    Jossey-Bass.

DuBois, D. L. & M. J. Karcher 2005 *Handbook of Youth Mentoring.*
    Thousand Oaks, Ca.: Sage Publications, Chapt. 19.

A partial list of some of Internet articles:
    Mentoring and Young People
    Mentoring for Vulnerable Young People
    Mentoring and attachment/ Ministry Magazine

[16] Creps, E.G. 2008 *Reverse Mentoring, How Young Leaders Can Transform
    the Church and why we should let them.* San Francisco, Ca.:
    Jossey-Bass.

[17] See, for example,
Kimmel, D.C. 1974 *Adulthood and Aging.* New York: John Wiley &
    Sons, Inc. p.26 ff.

[18] Three sources I found helpful in understanding postmodernism:

Smith, J.K.A. 2006 *Who is Afraid of PostModernism?* Grand Rapids,
    Michigan: Baker Academic.

Middleton R. & B.J. Walsh 1995 *Truth Is Stranger Than It Used To Be*. Downers Grove, Ill: Intervarsity Press.

Prickett, S. *Narrative Religion and Science, Fundamentalism versus Irony 1700-1999.*Cambridge, UK: Cambridge University Press chapters 1,6

[19] Kirk and Raven, 1963: 8-24

[20] Kirk and Raven, 1963; Kok, 1998: 31-38

[21] Armstrong, 1983; Kok, 1998: 38-43

[22] Armstrong, 1983; Kok, 1998: 43-51

[23] Armstrong 1983; Kok, 1998: 51-59

[24] Armstrong 1983; Kok, 1998: 60-69

[25] Armstrong 1983; Kok, 1998: 69-73

[26] Copleston, 1972: 17- 49

[27] Copleston, 1972

[28] Copleston, 1972: 225-229

[29] Copleston, 1960: 40

[30] Copleston, 1960

[31] Descartes 1637; van Rappard, 1967: 23

[32] Leibniz, 1714

[33] Wolff, 1713; van Rappard, 1976; Kant, 1902-1942; Fichte, 1794

[34] Copleston, 1960:135- 149

[35] Pascal, 1662; Copleston, 1958: 153-174

[36] Berlin, 1977

[37] Berlin, 1977

[38] Muller-Freienfels, 1938: 27-35; Lersch, 1960: 32, 39, 40, 67, 68; 79;
     Polkinghorne, 1983: 24-32

[39] Polkinghorne, 1983: 22

[40] Lersch, 1960: 33; Polkinghorne, 1983: 26

[41] Polkinghorne, 1983: 23

[42] Muller-Freienfels, 1938: 33; Lersch, 1960: 77

[43] Copleston, 1965: 371-372

INDEX

C.

critical of pomposity and hypocrisy 79
collaborative rather than competitive 79

D.
disconnects exists between generations 60
digital 4
doubt 12
dearth of ends rather than means 12
do-it-yourself project 14
Descartes, Rene 14 68
decade-long search for identity 17
disconnect between the generations 22
digital world 24
digitalized information 24
democratic 24
digitalized information 26
digitally shaped information 25
dictionary/ encyclopedia 25
democratization of culture 27
democratization of knowledge 27
discourse: easy going, colloquial , concrete 29
drink cheap beer 32
deliberate attempt at double-speak 36
Delores Park, Mission, San Francisco 38
dance between identity and relationship 47
Daloz-Parks 49
don't do anything for young people 51
distinguish development from history 53
development views people as of age 53
Duns Scotus 66
Dilthey 72
Droysen 74
disconnect between young and old 78
democratic and inclusive 79

E.
emerging adults 4 53 55
emerging generation 7

ABOUT THE AUTHOR

Harry Van Belle is a psychologist with a PhD degree in clinical psychology from the Free University of Amsterdam, The Netherlands. He has been a university professor, a practicing therapist, a workshop leader and a popular lecturer for more than 40 years. He has written extensively about topics related to stages of life, psychological development and psychotherapy. His career includes a stint as a supervisor of the psychology department in a psychiatric hospital, as the primary therapist of a counseling agency and as a professor of psychology in two Canadian university colleges. Since his retirement in 2000 he has devoted himself to writing and to mentoring emerging adults. He can be contacted at harryvanbelle@hotmail.com

CPSIA information can be obtained at www.ICGtesting.com
Printed in the USA
LVOW100918211012

303777LV00002B/1/P